THE INFORMATION CURE

· · · · · · · · · · · · · · · · · ·

Solving the Healthcare Crisis Systematically through Integrated Healthcare Management

By Jeff Margolis

Founder, Chairman and CEO of The TriZetto Group, Inc.

Library of Congress Control Number: 2009929103

The Information Cure: Solving the Healthcare Crisis Systematically through Integrated Healthcare Management / Jeff Margolis

ISBN: 978-1-60743-391-0

CONTENTS

• • • • • • • •

Foreword

If you're like most Americans, you were probably born in a hospital or other healthcare setting. Chances are good that you'll eventually die in a hospital or hospice care. Yet most Americans spend the entire time between birth and death confused about the very healthcare system in which life typically begins and ends.

One common misconception is that "the healthcare system" consists only of your hospital, your doctors' offices, and your pharmacy. However, these are only small parts of a much larger system, and most of us are unaware of just how many other elements of the system exist and how inextricably linked they are to one another. The interactions, shared information, and incentives among the parts of the system are what make the system run the way it does, warts and all. Understanding how the system works now can help us engineer it to work much more efficiently in the future. So how can you learn more about this vast and complicated system and—as part of the system yourself—how can you make it work better for you and your family?

For most of us, reading up on the healthcare system doesn't help clear away our confusion. Much of what has been written about the problems of the U.S. healthcare system is either about someone personally coping with a debilitating illness or—at the opposite end of the spectrum—general gloom and doom statistics or sweeping statements about social policy and healthcare reform. There is very little written in the way of concrete solutions that can be systematically implemented and that the average person can understand and apply.

Unlike other books lining bookstore shelves, this book is not about the high number of uninsured (although the lack of access to affordable health insurance is indisputably in need of attention); nor is it about the alleged failings of our government and private sector healthcare initiatives. Rather, this book addresses the more than 250 million Americans[i] who do have health coverage—the people who are connected to organized systems of benefits and care and who, nonetheless, spend the majority of their lives confused and frustrated about how to navigate the U.S. healthcare system.

My own experience with a serious chronic illness gave me an invaluable perspective on what it is like to be part of the U.S. healthcare system, and it became one catalyst for me to try to make our healthcare system work better. At age 19, I was diagnosed with Crohn's disease, an incurable, often painful disease that causes, among other things, chronic inflammation of the digestive tract. While in my prime, I was told that I would likely spend several weeks a year in the hospital and might not be able to have a conventional career. For me, this prognosis created motivation instead of fear, and I tried to "outrun" both the pain of the disease and the prognosis. When my illness was diagnosed, I happened to be in college, studying management information systems. I was learning how to apply information and develop systematic approaches to different industries. As my career initially developed in the information systems consulting business, I was exposed to methods of applying systems science and information technology to solve complex problems in energy, mining, banking, manufacturing and distribution, pharmaceuticals, and healthcare delivery. I was fortunate to be at the forefront at a time when the application of information technology to improve business processes was starting to enter the mainstream. Ironically, just as I was determining to focus my career energies on the most complex of these industries—healthcare—my illness worsened and the two paths converged.

Beginning at age 27, and over the next seven years, I had seven abdominal surgeries, including the removal of my colon. In the span of 48 hours during one of my hospital stays at a prestigious teaching hospital, I was twice given medication to which I had a severe allergic reaction, even though my medical chart indicated that that particular drug should not be administered. Although some of the surgeries had positive outcomes, some did not. I experienced many of the flaws of the healthcare system: poor coordination among providers, high cost, and inadequate systems for communicating key information about medication allergies—a failure that sometimes proves fatal. As I navigated the system as a patient, even with my considerable experience in the industry at that time, it became clear how incomprehensible and inefficient our healthcare system was. However, it was equally evident that there was an abundance of excellent system components that made me feel very fortunate to be receiving my care in our country. I knew the resources being applied to help me were far less available, if available at all, in many other countries.

So, after implementing information management systems in multiple industries and serving as chief information officer (CIO) of several healthcare payer organizations, some of which ran hospitals, clinics, and pharmacies as well, I wondered why no one had yet applied a comprehensive systematic approach to healthcare. I decided to create a company with a mission to help enable a more capable, organized system of benefits and care.

My experience as a patient continues to inform my work, but it is the combination of that experience and my education and professional qualifications that gives me a unique perspective. As a former CIO of healthcare payer and provider organizations and in my current role as Chairman and CEO of The TriZetto Group, a healthcare information technology company that supplies solutions that link benefits and care for more than 100 million people, I know the significant improvements that systematically applied technology can bring to the healthcare system. Today, at the age of 46, I make sure my work is informed by serving on the Board of Directors for Hoag Memorial Hospital Presbyterian; on the Board of Governors of Cedars-Sinai Hospital in California; on the national board of the Crohn's & Colitis Foundation of America; and as an advisory member for the Center for Healthcare Policy and Research at the University of California, Irvine. I have seen and continue to see firsthand the complex array of healthcare issues challenging patients, doctors, insurers, researchers, and others. Finally, my training in management information systems bolsters my ability to look at healthcare from a systems science point of view. This combined experience has compelled me to ask: How do all of the parts of the healthcare system interact? And what is it about those interactions that leads to the poorly coordinated communication, lack of efficiency, and skyrocketing healthcare costs we are seeing today?

This book is intended to explain in terms that anyone can understand how our healthcare system works and why it has the flaws it does, while also conveying that the problems of affordability and inefficiency plastering the headlines are absolutely solvable. Since we are part of the system ourselves, there are things we can do to improve our healthcare experience. We all need to play a more active role in making healthcare decisions based on cost and quality. And we need to start budgeting for healthcare, much as we do for retirement, especially as employers shift more of the cost responsibility to consumers. But regardless of what we do, the system must be designed to give consumers like us better information with which to make healthcare decisions as well as to provide tools for saving, just as actively managed retirement plans help people save for retirement.

Any problem passively ignored is likely to get worse. The key to taking action as a healthcare consumer is knowing how things work. Reading this book is an important step in understanding how the U.S. healthcare system functions today and how it can and should be transformed.

• • • • • • • • • • • • •

CHAPTER ONE

Taking a Systems Approach

The whole is more than the sum of its parts.
– Aristotle

Does the U.S. healthcare system need a "do not resuscitate" order? Is it beyond repair? When you read the newspapers, watch TV, go to the Internet, ask your neighbor (or better yet, your doctor or pharmacist), you might think our health-care system is among the worst in the world. Some of the more endlessly cited statistics depict Uncle Sam as an under-performer because the United States famously posts poorer longevity and higher infant mortality scores than other developed countries.

Statistics, however, don't tell the whole story. Often they are used pedantically to pound an agenda. I, for one, don't believe that the statistics that rank the United States so poorly are tabulated with equivalent levels of precision across the globe. To begin with, the statistical playing field is not level. Because we operate with third-party payers (insurers) that require highly accurate data for payment, we capture and report much more information than is captured in countries where providers are paid a fixed salary. What is actually reported in these countries tends to make their healthcare systems look better than they would if more comprehensive data were reported.

Second, some of our most disenfranchised patients, whether citizens or not, tend to receive much of their healthcare in emergency rooms because they either cannot afford or do not have a primary care doctor. In addition, they forgo routine screenings and generally fail to take care of healthcare needs as they arise. Instead, these individuals seek care in the emergency room when their healthcare needs have become so serious that they have little other choice.

It so happens that U.S. emergency rooms are one of the places where we capture statistical information with great precision and where both media and public interests are often directed. When you combine patients who have received poor prior care with the high-cost setting of an ER, you get a skewed perspective on the U.S. healthcare system.

Third, and more important than statistical precision or where statistics are gathered, however, is the substance of what we're measuring and reporting. Measuring and publicizing our country's healthcare system primarily by birth and death endpoints leaves out all of the healthcare people get in between, which includes some of the best care in the world. But based on the high accuracy of U.S. healthcare data relative to many other countries, the location where healthcare data are often gathered, and the specific healthcare measures that are tracked, you could easily reach a very different conclusion about the state of our healthcare system.

It's reasonable to assume that if we were to look at these statistics only for those who are part of an organized system of care—that is, people who have health insurance—U.S. healthcare might score very high marks. This is because many of the individual elements of the U.S. healthcare system actually are in fine shape. We have highly trained physicians, nurses, and other medical professionals who are sought after by people in other countries as well as our own; we also have an abundance of first-rate medical facilities, state-of-the-art medical equipment technology, and effective and innovative drugs and other biotechnologies. But my point—and one of the main points of this book—is that the way in which the parts of the U.S. healthcare system interact or fail to interact is the real problem, not the medical care providers, the insurance companies, the relative amount of money spent on healthcare, the pharmaceutical companies, or even U.S. healthcare social policy itself.

Understanding the systems approach

What is a system?

A system is a combination of elements and behaviors that interact to achieve an objective.

In order to improve our healthcare system, we first need to understand the components of that system and how they work together. So what is the U.S. healthcare system anyway? Indeed, what is a system? It seems that systems are popping up everywhere—and not just in healthcare. We have transportation systems, food distribution systems, and even home entertainment systems. There is actually a discipline of systems science, although few people study it. The late C. W. Churchman, an esteemed professor at the University of California, Berkeley from 1957 to 1996, was one of the first to define a "systems approach" to solving problems. While systematic thinking can and should include social policy, my experience is that when people throw up their hands and rely primarily upon policy intervention to solve a tough problem, it is usually due to a lack of systematic discipline. This is clear in the U.S. financial system as well as in the healthcare system.

When you study systems, you are often first introduced to the concept of home heating. Understanding a simple closed system like home heating is a good way to begin to understand a bit about systems science and—as we will see later—how systems science can be applied to fix the U.S. healthcare system. The basic elements of a typical home heating system are the air in your home, the thermostat, and the furnace. The thermostat sets the target, measures the air temperature, and, if required, sends a signal to the furnace that in turn heats and circulates the air. When the air achieves the desired temperature, the furnace shuts off. It's a simple and perfect closed system as long as you know what you want the temperature to be. Well, almost perfect.

Suppose it's hotter outside than you want the temperature inside to be, and now you need to reduce the temperature inside your house. To do so, you need to add another element—the element of cooling—to the system if you want to achieve your target. Now the thermostat has to be intelligent enough to tell the furnace when to go on or off, when to tell the air conditioner to go on or off, and when to tell both to do nothing. This is where many college students decide to study philosophy, because they are smart enough to know it only gets more complicated. For example, what about the air itself? How efficiently does it move around? What about humidity? Are the windows open? Should we cool the part of the house facing the sun and heat the part facing away from the sun to achieve the greatest efficiency? Designing a comprehensive heating and cooling system can become overwhelming if you consider every possible variable, so it is important to focus your energy on the variables that matter most. The same is true for designing any system, including one as massive as healthcare.

Systems thinking meets the healthcare system

In terms of the healthcare system, let me assure you that there is little common understanding today of what elements compose it and how each is supposed to affect the others. Many people erroneously think of the healthcare system as only the elements they can see and touch: their doctor's office, the hospital, and their local pharmacy. But there is much more to the healthcare system than that. If you believe that your highly skilled physician is an expert concerning the healthcare system in its entirety, then you should also believe that your first-rate auto mechanic is an expert in the automotive and transportation industries. Most people intuitively know that even though their superstar mechanic has specialized knowledge of particular makes and models of automobiles, and perhaps even specializes in transmissions, he or she is probably not qualified to run Toyota Motor Corporation.

Similarly, healthcare specialists are systems experts on a subset of closed human systems, such as the digestive system, the circulatory system, or the nervous system. As more medical research yields deeper understanding of smaller and more discrete anatomical systems and the forces of man and nature that can disrupt them, physicians and medical researchers naturally move toward specialization. As these physicians expand their knowledge about treating patients within particular specialties, they understandably have less time to focus on how the whole system ties together. Herein lies a paradox of systems thinking—and a problem in today's healthcare delivery system. On the one hand, if you have a medical problem involving the microscopic workings of your inner ear, then you are thankful that there are specialists who pursue their understanding of that anatomical system to the nth degree. On the other hand, the fact that these specialists are able to solve your complex ear problem does not necessarily mean they understand the framework of the entire healthcare system. Furthermore, if that specialized knowledge is either unknown or inaccessible to those who could benefit from it, it becomes isolated and useless to the system.

Thankfully, there are some physicians, typically called primary care doctors, who concentrate their careers on understanding how all the different anatomical and certain psychological and social systems interact with and affect one another. These days, however, fewer and fewer medical students are choosing to become primary care doctors. Ironically, despite being trained to understand the total human being, both psychologically and physiologically, primary care doctors are not as well compensated as their specialized peers. The parallel irony is that just as you cannot efficiently deploy the relatively advanced components of home heating and cooling systems without a thermostat, it is similarly difficult to effectively deploy sophisticated components of the healthcare system (such as specialty care) without primary care doctors.

If the trend of more medical students choosing careers in specialty care continues, the United States could end up with the healthcare equivalent of too few "thermostats" to signal when the heating and cooling elements should go on and off. Primary care doctors are an essential control mechanism for the health of the patient, much the same way that thermostats are the control mechanism for the temperature of the house. Their understanding of the many variables that can affect the health of their patients qualifies primary care doctors to make smart decisions in consultation with their patients about when to "turn on" visits to specialists and other care settings beyond the primary care doctor's office.

For the house with no thermostat, the result might be either too high a temperature and lots of expensive wasted energy, or too low a temperature, which could cause the pipes to freeze and avoidable leaks to spring up. For the patient with no primary care doctor or accurate alternative information source, the result might be either too many unnecessary tests and visits to specialists and a resulting increase in healthcare costs, or not enough diagnostic tests and visits to specialists when these services are needed. In addition, the patient could spend more time in pain and run a greater risk that his illness or injury could become very serious or, perhaps, deadly.

Clearly, primary care doctors (as well as specialists) play a central role in American healthcare. But it is important to realize that they represent only one element of the healthcare system—albeit a very sacred one. Doctors and other providers have their hands full with the system elements they need to know in order to provide care to human beings. They cannot possibly know the whole healthcare system, nor should you assume that they do.

Managing through measuring: the basics of information technology

So, how do goal-seeking human beings today think about taming complex systems, such as healthcare, so they can better understand and manage them? Nearly anything that can be observed or measured that, in turn, would lead to a specified action (e.g., if the temperature is too low, then turn on the furnace) can be expressed as a mathematical or rules-based algorithm. The ability to capture measurements or values in digital form, process those data against a set of instructions, or algorithms, and do something with the results is the backbone of modern information technology.

The world seems full of jargon about information technology, so let's make it easier to understand. Software is simply rules; hardware simply determines how much data can be stored and how fast it can be processed; and networks simply determine how quickly it can be transported. The challenge in information technology—including its applicability to healthcare—is assessing how best to use software, hardware, and networks to facilitate the achievement of specific objectives. In healthcare information technology, examples can range from deriving a clinical diagnosis that requires dozens of inputs with hundreds of permutations (for which the human brain is still the reigning supercomputer champion) to simple algorithms, such as a health plan's checking to see if a physician filled out a diagnosis code before reimbursing him for an office visit, or whether a prescription has been written and filled.

The press is full of stories about doctors being unfairly buried in administrative duties. However, before you express outrage that a physician should have to waste valuable time filling in a diagnosis code properly to get paid, keep in mind that failure to properly record a medication, test, or diagnosis could result in an allergic or adverse drug interaction, the unnecessary duplication of a particular test, or a delayed or incorrect diagnosis. And so, if you begin to think about it systematically—a habit I hope you will pick up from this book—administrative data used to receive accurate payment in one context may be used as important clinical data in another. If you need medical care in the future and the doctor treating you does not know about the data from past tests, diagnoses, and medications, you might wish that the doctor had access to your health history in a digital (i.e., computer-accessible) form so she could see all of the care you have received. In Chapter Nine, we'll examine ways of developing a health information aggregation of patient information and how that information can be used to increase quality of medical care and reduce cost.

Information underload

There is a wealth of data being captured every day about who gets what healthcare and how much it costs, but because it is fragmented and much of it is captured manually (not digitally) on those long paper forms you fill out every time you go to the doctor, it is not being used in the most effective way or shared among the different parts of the healthcare system in order to help it run effectively. Stories abound about people ill on vacation receiving a drug to which they are allergic, simply because the information about the drug allergy was locked up in a paper-based file at their physician's office, instead of being available where patients and providers need it.

Similarly, if you move to a new city or simply switch doctors, your medical record is not automatically transferred, and when it is, it's often in the form of manila folders, stuffed with non-standard forms in messy handwriting. As a result, the new provider has no practical way of knowing anything about your medical history, medications, allergies, past diagnostic tests, or risk factors unless you remember to include every detail on the new provider's paper form. This lack of information can lead doctors to order tests that have already been done, prescribe medication that can interact negatively with others you are taking, and lead to countless other problems ranging from mere inconvenience or unnecessary expense to a dangerous drug interaction or misdiagnosis. However, this type of information deficiency is not the doctor's fault, nor is it yours. The system simply was not engineered to assemble and distribute information to the greatest benefit of providers and patients. By the way, simply digitizing a system that is not well engineered to begin with is proverbially known in the information technology world as "paving cow paths." Computerizing a flawed process simply speeds it up but does not fix it. That is why you and your doctor should be wary about claims that the implementation of electronic health records alone will dramatically improve care or save money. Unless the processes and technology are engineered together, it won't.

Coordination among system parts

The nice thing about systems that are truly understood is that the major elements do not change. What can change, however, is our knowledge of what elements compose the whole system and the way in which those elements interact and coordinate with one another. That is where the potential for improvement lies. In a well-designed, engineered, and organized system, the whole should be greater than the sum of its parts.

The result of a well-designed system should be better than any individual piece because the parts work together in a systematic way to create synergy. Let's use a trip to Las Vegas as an example. The fact that you can hop in your car and go to Las Vegas (assuming you live on the mainland) is the sum of a transportation system that links various parts together in an organized way. Some of the major system elements are: roads and the people who build them; cars and the people who make them; gas stations and the people who work in them; oil-producing countries and the entities that refine oil into gasoline; and people and companies who sell food so that you can eat along the way.

As a consumer, you can navigate this system smoothly so it is easy to take it for granted. Because of the way the parts work together, you can do exactly what you need to do when and how you choose to do it. The system as a whole allows you to accomplish more than if you simply experienced just one part of the system, such as driving in your car (but not being able to eat dinner or stop at a restroom along the way), or eating at a restaurant (but not having a car and road to get you to Las Vegas). However, what if, instead of being made of smoothed asphalt or concrete, "all roads leading to Vegas" were train tracks but your car still had the standard four rubber tires? Not only would the road and your car not be designed to go together, but they would actually end up working against each other. Of course, this example would occur only if the railroad company owned all the land routes to Vegas and the mere notion of cars threatened its survival.

Ludicrous as it may seem, this is how parts of the U.S. healthcare system are currently designed. Although many of the individual parts are excellent, the system as a whole is *less* than the sum of those parts. At the most fundamental level, there is poor communication among the parts of the system. Information is not shared among the various elements to allow them to get what they need when they need it, and much of the information exists in paper form instead of systematically being entered into a computer so it can be shared in digital form. To make matters worse, many of the healthcare system's well-intended financial incentives and penalties end up rewarding the wrong behaviors and do not encourage behaviors that would lead to better health, better treatment, and fewer dollars spent. Just as the train track and rubber tires would work against each other on a trip to Vegas, so do many parts of the U.S. healthcare system confound the consumer.

The system through a wider lens

So why have we failed to structure the system so the interactions among the parts add value for the users of the system and work in harmony to take us smoothly down the healthcare highway to our intended destination? How can we take a systems science approach to solving the problems of the U.S. healthcare system? Systematically re-engineering the U.S. healthcare system will require us to broaden our view of what is included in the system and to go beyond the doctor's office, the hospital, and the pharmacy. Let's take some examples of things we do every day. Is going to the grocery store part of the healthcare system? What about your daily hygiene and exercise routine? Is taking time off from work for vacation part of the healthcare system? How about looking up generic healthcare information online? All of these behaviors can have a major influence on our health, yet if asked what composes that system, few of us would intuitively include them as part of the organized U.S. healthcare system.

How about your health plan benefits? Are they part of the healthcare system? When you fill out the enrollment form for your health plan each year, do you think about how your choice of benefits will affect how much you pay for care as well as which providers you can see? Because most of us get healthcare coverage through our employer (who pays the majority of the premium cost), many of us take it for granted and feel entitled to receive health benefits. We don't think of the benefit plan as part of the healthcare system because access to this healthcare coverage has always been provided to us. But it is an important piece and one we need to think about carefully because the specific benefit plan we choose (or are assigned) is the organizing principal that affects both our cost and quality of care.

Taking a systems approach means we need to have the most complete picture possible of all of the parts of the system and then structure the interactions among the parts to give everyone who uses the system what they need. There are three primary repositories of data that can be turned into useful systematic information.

The first is core benefit administration (insurers' central administration systems that support all transactions related to enrollment, contracting, claims payment, customer service, and more). The second is care management (member health information and content that facilitates the member health management processes). The third repository is constituent information (including demographics, preferences, and other volunteered information that facilitates constructive interaction among healthcare constituents, particularly between providers and consumers). In most geographic areas health plans are best positioned to systematically coordinate these three types of information repositories on behalf of the consumer. In select geographies, integrated provider delivery systems are equally well positioned to facilitate the same type of coordination.

Integrated Healthcare Management is key

Contrary to the pessimistic tone adopted by the media and politicians, the ills of the U.S. healthcare system are eminently curable if we treat them systematically. I call this systematic view Integrated Healthcare Management (IHM). IHM takes the best knowledge we have for managing benefits and the best knowledge we have for managing care and systematically coordinates it in an optimal way for the healthcare consumer. If we can make the right information available wherever and whenever consumers (patients), providers, employers, and brokers need it, and carefully craft behavioral incentives for people at every level of the system, we can reduce costs, improve quality, and make our healthcare system an example for the rest of the world. In other words, the U.S. healthcare system may not be on the brink of failure, but rather on the brink of unparalleled success.

The first step in improving a system is to understand why it doesn't work. In Chapter Two, The Blind Men and the Elephant: Lessons for Healthcare, we will see the sheer enormity of the U.S. healthcare system and why experiencing and understanding the entire system has been challenging for doctors, patients, and policymakers.

CHAPTER TWO

● ● ● ● ● ● ● ● ● ● ● ● ●

The Blind Men and the Elephant:
Lessons for Healthcare

*The wise man laughed as he turned and walked home. For he,
himself, had once been as foolish as the others, thinking he knew
what an elephant was like by simply touching one of its parts.*

From the parable The Blind Men and the Elephant[2]

Understanding how the U.S. healthcare system works is a monumental task. Its vast scale and tremendous complexity have baffled rocket scientists and brain surgeons alike. The sheer size of the healthcare system is mind-boggling. We have over 815,000 doctors[3] in the United States. More than 3,000 hospitals throughout the country handle roughly 72 million admissions per year.[4] Approximately 3.8 billion prescriptions were bought in 2007[5] from the roughly 2,100 registered pharmaceuticals on the market. In addition, more than 3 billion medical claims are processed each year. Americans spent $2.4 trillion on healthcare in 2008, accounting for 17 percent of the gross domestic product.[6] Given these numbers, it is no surprise that the average consumer has, at best, a cursory understanding of only a few parts of this enormous system. Add to these figures the amount of time, energy, and expertise involved in developing and managing all of the parts of the system, and it's no wonder our healthcare system is so hard to figure out. Policymakers could spend a lifetime trying to understand how the entire system works, but they don't have that luxury. Based upon my personal interactions with members of Congress, the typical lawmaker is barraged with such a broad range of topics that, even with the help of specialized staff, it's amazing they can keep healthcare on their Top Ten list. Yet understanding the whole system is the first step toward systematically engineering it to improve quality while lowering costs, and helping the system to better serve you and your family.

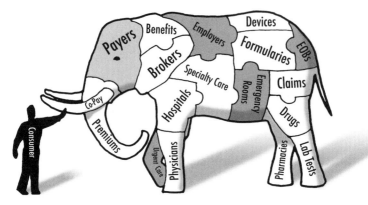

The well-known parable of the Blind Men and the Elephant illustrates the impossibility of any person's getting to know the entire healthcare animal. This ancient metaphor has many different versions, but the basic story is this:

There once was a walled-in city where all of the inhabitants were blind. One day, a king stopped by with his entourage and camped on the outskirts of the city. He was accompanied by a large elephant, which he used to frighten his enemies away. Six blind men—each regarded as highly knowledgeable among their people—hurried out to "see" what the elephant was like. The first man, upon feeling the elephant's trunk, said, "This creature is long like a snake." The second man accidentally collided with the elephant's broad side. He exclaimed, "This beast is like a big wall—smooth and strong." The third man was nearly skewered by the elephant's tusk. Grimacing in pain, he said, "This animal is pointy and sharp like a spear. I see why the king's enemies keep their distance!" He ran away in fright. The fourth blind man reached down and found the elephant's leg, which was rough and dimpled. At that moment, the elephant stomped his foot, sending the blind man flying. The man said, "This elephant is like a moving tree trunk. It strikes the ground with a mighty force." Off he ran to join the others. The fifth man grabbed at the elephant's tail. "This animal can't scare anyone away. It is merely a frayed piece of rope." He walked off casually toward the city. The sixth man rushed out to see what the excitement was about. He felt the elephant's thin ear flapping in the breeze. "Wow! This creature is delicate just like a fan," he exclaimed.

Finally, a truly wise man came and walked slowly around the elephant, taking his time and studying the elephant thoroughly from all sides. He touched every part of it, listening to its sounds and smelling the elephant. After finding its mouth and feeding it a treat, he returned to the city. There he discovered the six blind men arguing about what the elephant was like. "It's like a snake," said one man. "No, it's like a wall," said another. "It's sharp like a spear," said a third man. "No, it's like a tree trunk," retorted another man. "No, it's like a rope," insisted another. "It's like a fan," said the last man. The wise man laughed as he turned and walked home. For he, himself, had once been as foolish as the others, thinking he knew what an elephant was like by simply touching one of its parts.

Feeling our way in the dark

It is easy to see how this parable applies to the healthcare system. Think of the healthcare system as a huge elephant with each body part a different element, such as doctors, pharmaceutical companies, hospitals, pharmacies, medical equipment, consumers (patients), brokers, employers, and payers (the insurance companies that collect premiums and pay claims). Although many of us are not literally blind as in the parable, it often seems as if we are feeling our way through a dark jungle where our ability to fully see and comprehend the huge healthcare beast in front of us is severely impaired. Like the blind men in the parable, we as consumers each experience only small parts of the whole healthcare system—and solely in the narrow context of our own interactions. The result is a myopic view, rather than a thorough, systematic understanding of all parts of the U.S. healthcare system and how they interact with one another.

Here's an example. Imagine meeting the healthcare beast for the first time, perhaps in your first job. This encounter may be through an employer during an "open enrollment" period (or, if you are self-insured, directly through your health plan). Like the blind men, you touch this part of the healthcare animal and form an impression. You might perceive the healthcare system as a long form you must complete; choices you must make about which benefits, doctors, and hospitals you will be able to access; and a big, fat payroll deduction about to gobble up your hard-earned paycheck. But missing from your picture of the healthcare system are many other pieces of information, such as the likely actual cost of each procedure or test you need during the year or throughout your lifetime, how the hospital and networks of doctors run their businesses, and how brokers may advise your employer about what health plan and group of benefits it should offer. You also may not have realized how the parts of the system are connected. For example, when you filled out the enrollment form at your first job, did you think about the fact that if you had to switch employers someday, you'd likely have to switch health plans, which might mean leaving the doctors you had gotten to know and trust?

Once enrolled in the health plan, you would typically make an appointment with your primary care doctor. From this interaction, you begin to see the healthcare system as a provider of basic care, a source of information, a giver of referrals to specialists, and a place to read hours' worth of magazines you would ordinarily never pick up. However, there is much of the healthcare system you still can't see, such as whether the doctor or nurses know anything about you until you are actually in a room together; how your doctor is paid by the health plan for the care you received; the network of hospitals and diagnostic centers with which your physician is affiliated; the criteria your doctor will use to decide if you need a referral to a specialist; and the list of approved drugs your health plan will cover (called a formulary).

As you venture further into the healthcare system, the jungle around you seems to become darker and darker. You play a bit too much tennis one weekend and return to work with a case of tennis elbow. You try to find a specialist for your elbow, but you struggle for weeks to get an appointment. You finally track down an orthopedist who has an available appointment within this decade. When you arrive at the orthopedist's office, you are told that your referral from the primary care doctor was not received and you will need to sign a coverage waiver and pay for the visit out of pocket. After reading more magazines, you are led into an exam room where the specialist examines you for a period of time much briefer than your wait. The doctor then asks the nurse to prepare an order for you to receive an X-ray, just to be sure something more serious is not in play. After you go to the diagnostic center, having read still more magazines (which is okay because you can't have your mobile phone on) and having had the X-ray taken, you are able to arrange a follow-up appointment with the orthopedist with amazing efficiency compared to your first visit. The physician, having ruled out a more severe diagnosis, develops a treatment plan complete with physical therapy and a prescription for painkillers and anti-inflammatory medications. You now perceive the healthcare system as a long search for a specialist; poor communication between your doctor's office and the specialist's office; an obligation to pay for care that should have been covered; an interminable wait to see the specialist; a professional but very short examination; a visit to a diagnostic center; an efficient follow-up visit and another referral—this time, for physical therapy—and at long last a prescription to alleviate your symptoms.

Enormity and complexity challenge consumers

By now, you have interacted with several different parts of the healthcare animal—your employer, your primary care doctor, and now this specialist. You may think you are developing quite a comprehensive image of the healthcare system despite the darkness that engulfs you. But what you don't see is the complexity of orthopedics or of specialty care in general. You saw a general orthopedist, but there are also orthopedists who specialize in hip or knee replacements; others who specialize in hands and fingers; and so it goes for many parts of the body except, perhaps, a broken eyelash. There are nearly 150 medical specialties and sub-specialties. If orthopedics alone is so complex and specialized, imagine how difficult it would be for anyone to know the whole healthcare system or even to understand all that relates just to delivering care. As we learned in Chapter One, the healthcare system comprises not only delivery of care but also benefits administrators (health plans or payers) as well as the individuals, or constituents, who use the system—consumers, providers, employers, and brokers. Even with the interactions you have accumulated, you have barely scratched the surface of the healthcare system.

As you advance deeper into the dark jungle, you see other parts of the healthcare elephant. For example, when you fill your prescriptions at the local pharmacy, you start to view the healthcare system as a collector of co-payments, a giver of the medication your doctor prescribed, and maybe even a provider of instructions on when to take the drug. But you don't see the complex research and development organ inside the healthcare animal, which invented, tested, and brought your drugs to market. It is also unlikely that you know the actual retail cost of the drugs you receive, because you pay only a small fraction of the total cost—your co-payments. And while you are waiting for your prescriptions, you are probably unaware that the pharmacist is checking your eligibility (whether your health plan covers these particular prescription drugs) and your co-payment amounts against a computer database from your health plan or the pharmacy benefits manager hired by the health plan. In this situation, you never experience the parts of the elephant responsible for paying for most of your prescription—the health plan and the employer. Like the blind men, you see only one part of the whole.

Also like the blind men, consumers may have very different impressions about what the healthcare system is because their interactions even with the same part of the system may vary. For example, if you have a mail-order prescription benefit and your prescription doesn't arrive at your house on time, you may view the healthcare system as an inefficient, bureaucratic impediment to getting the medicine you need. However, if your prescription appears on your doorstep just when you expect it, you'll probably think the healthcare system is a well-oiled machine that just saved you a trip to the pharmacy. Such is the result when people think of one small part or one limited interaction as the whole system.

Seeing the whole system: Is it possible?
We've seen how consumers develop a narrow view of the healthcare system from touching only a few parts of the whole. Similarly, the other parts of the system, such as doctors, physician assistants, nurses, physical therapists, pharmacists, hospital professionals, and employers also touch only a few other parts of the system and can also be likened to the blind men in the parable. And while any one of these parts of the healthcare system may be an expert in its own processes and procedures, each knows little about the rest of the system, and some have no idea the other parts exist. For example, your pharmacist interacts with patients, doctors, hospitals and payers, but may never touch the brokers or employers. And his experiences with the parts he does touch are limited. He sees patients as receivers of medications; the health plan as the giver of permission; the doctor or physician extender as an authorized entity that orders prescriptions; but never sees these parts in their entirety as they relate to one another.

Similarly, while your primary care doctor may be an expert in internal medicine, if you need surgery, have a heart problem, cancer, or an issue with your lungs or endocrine system, your doctor will likely need to refer you to a specialist. Just learning internal medicine took years of medical school, an exhausting internship and residency, and years of experience treating patients. Despite this arduous training, it would be unreasonable to expect your doctor to be an expert in every specialty or to have as thorough an understanding of the other parts of the elephant, especially those she may never touch directly, such as employers, brokers, and payers.

As with the blind men trying to get a complete understanding of the elephant but describing it in entirely different ways, we, too, may think we fully understand the healthcare system based simply on repeated encounters with one, or even several, small parts. However, the healthcare system simply has too many parts, each of which is too large and complex for every part to fully know all of the others. Because of the enormity and complexity of the U.S. healthcare system, it is virtually impossible for any patient or provider to understand it as one organism. And why should they try to understand a whole system when what they really care about is whether their own interactions with the system give them what they need?

We all know the U.S. healthcare system is not performing up to its full potential. However, until we consistently start to treat healthcare as a system, in its true definition, with knowledge of all the parts and how they work together, we will not be able to tame this unruly beast and get it to do what we need it to do. Up to now, much energy has been focused on trying to fix a particular part of the system perceived at any given time by policymakers to be the biggest problem. But this approach leaves out the interactions among the parts. Improving just one part of the system without considering how the other parts interact will not necessarily make the system work more efficiently; just as constructing a state-of-the-art train track would do nothing to help the car with rubber tires in Chapter One move from one place to another.

When is a system really a system?
By the time you finish this book, you will have a basic understanding of the parts of the U.S. healthcare system. You will also understand that in most areas of the country the U.S. healthcare "system" is not an organized system at all. In order to successfully navigate the healthcare jungle, you need to understand that the system is disconnected and that often there is no one person or entity making sure you get all of the care and information you need. In other words, there is no healthcare equivalent of the "wise man" in the fable (although there are some entities striving to become wiser). Simply knowing that no single entity completely understands the system should make you realize that you need to become a more active participant in your own healthcare. And, once you are active instead of passive, you can seek the most effective elements of the system with the greatest level of efficiency and results.

Looking at how other industries have successfully engineered or re-engineered their systems to achieve the best possible outcome may shed light on our attempt to improve the U.S. healthcare system. In Chapter Three, we will travel down the road with one automotive company that successfully applied technology and systems engineering principles to create a state-of-the-art system for production, care and maintenance while delivering higher quality for less cost. Sadly, this is a feat that our healthcare system has yet to accomplish on any broad scale for humans.

• • • • • • • • • • • • • •

The Lexus and the Human*

*It's a funny thing about life: If you refuse to accept
anything but the very best you very often get it.*

– Somerset Maugham

Which would you rather be: a Lexus or a human being? The answer may seem obvious. A human enjoys free will, the pursuit of happiness, and many other privileges we hold dear, while the Lexus is simply a car at the mercy of whoever ends up in the driver's seat. But if you have ever seen how easily a Lexus is able to be "treated" for an "illness" and how thorough and transferable its communications-linked maintenance records are in comparison to the fragmented paper-based medical records at your doctors' offices, you might just opt to be a Lexus.

In 1992, I purchased a Lexus LS400. At the time, Lexus advertised that no matter which Lexus dealer you took your car to for service, that dealer would know about you and how to take care of your car because the service records from its entire dealer network were linked through a satellite network. Given my interest in systems engineering and information technology, I was intrigued by this pioneering attempt to systematize how routine service and repairs were tracked and provided. Also, because I had done information systems consulting work in the manufacturing industry, I was curious as to whether the emerging claims of applying information technology to improve both the ownership experience and the driving experience held up in reality.

To my delight, the advertising claims were actually true. Despite the fact that the Internet was not readily available to the general public in 1992, Lexus had

*With literary apologies to Thomas L. Friedman, whose writing I greatly admire.

made use of the best technology available at the time for this application—satellite-linked networks—and used it to give consumers and dealers the information they needed where and when they needed it. Further, they had built information sensors into the car itself that, when connected to the network by technicians, could help diagnose and fix problems when they occurred. To this day, any Lexus dealer can access the service record of any Lexus and see what services have been performed, whether the Lexus needs an oil change, is due for a 75,000-mile checkup, or could use a brake replacement. Lexus was the first in its field to implement this type of standardized service system across locations. Unsurprisingly, it fast became the standard for the automotive industry.

Lexus links information for repair and maintenance . . .
Lexus' communications-linked maintenance system works well not only for the owner of the Lexus (the consumer) but also gives the authorized service technician (the provider) valuable information he or she can use to best service the car. The technician is prompted as to what services to perform for a routine maintenance "checkup" and he "treats" the Lexus based on standard established practices for a car model of that particular Lexus' condition and age. Once those services are performed, the technician electronically records

exactly what was done so next time the car needs repairs, any certified Lexus technician will be able to pick up where the last person left off. When the car needs repairs (has an illness or injury), the technician can see what diagnostic procedures have already been done, thereby avoiding unnecessary duplication or waste, such as changing the oil twice in three months. The technician also has access to information about the Lexus' warranty (analogous to the health insurance coverage for a human), allowing both the car owner and the dealer to know up front which services the car owner will have to pay for out of pocket and which will be covered. This means the service technician is also able to give an accurate pricing estimate for work before it is performed and an accurate bill when the work is completed. Finally, the Lexus has a proactive reminder system for letting a Lexus owner know when to take the vehicle in for routine maintenance such as an oil change.

... while fragmentation plagues human care

In stark contrast to Lexus' systematic way of maintaining and repairing its cars, the U.S. healthcare system lacks the coordination to care for humans as reliably and comprehensively. Although the human race has been around much longer than the Lexus, and even though a luxury automobile is just an inanimate object, the Lexus enjoys a much higher degree of precision regarding its care. For starters, our system does not reliably enable providers and consumers to access medical records wherever and whenever we need them. Each doctor's office keeps information relating only to that doctor's treatment of a particular patient, and in most cases it is handwritten so it can't be transmitted easily to another doctor or hospital. As a result, the same diagnostic tests are often performed unknowingly by different doctors on the same patient, driving up the cost of medical care and wasting the patient's time on a test he or she has already had. In some cases, this lack of medical record availability can lead to more serious consequences. For example, if you are unconscious and are delivered by ambulance to an emergency room, the doctors and nurses might inadvertently give you a drug to which you are allergic, because they can't access your medical record. To add insult to injury, once you are released from the emergency room, there is no guarantee that documentation of the treatment you just received will be sent to your primary care doctor to be entered into your medical record.

Not only are we humans unable to access our medical records when needed, but there is a tremendous degree of variation in the treatment we receive, even among people with the same condition and similar health backgrounds. Treatment of humans, unlike the Lexus, is not consistently based on "best practices" for a particular condition. In fact, according to an array of medical research studies, including the seminal Dartmouth Atlas of Health Care,[7] which initially published research from Dr. Jack Wennberg, there are glaring variations in how medical resources are distributed and used in the United States, including widespread unwarranted variation from what is deemed by healthcare research experts to be the best practice in a particular situation. This variation is the root of deficiencies in quality and inefficiencies in cost and can have severe, sometimes deadly, implications for patients. For example, there is agreement within the medical community that, following a heart attack, patients who can tolerate them should be given beta-blockers (a class of pharmaceutical drugs) to lower the risk of recurrence. Yet, even though this is almost as basic a step as making sure the oil filter is replaced during an oil change, the compliance rate in a benchmark study in 1995 (three years after I bought my Lexus) ranged between five percent and 85 percent depending on the particular provider. How would you like to be one of the patients whose doctor was unaware of this well-researched and inexpensive treatment protocol or was under the false belief that it wasn't important? And further, in a question to be raised later in this book, should doctors who don't adhere to established best practices be reimbursed differently from those who do?

In contrast to the Lexus' easily available warranty, which shows both consumers and dealers what services are covered, in our healthcare system providers do not always know what services are covered for their human patients. Moreover, patients often only know the co-payment amount instead of the total cost of a given procedure, and many are unaware of the large monthly contribution employers pay toward the health insurance premium.

In addition, humans, unlike the Lexus, generally do not have a reliable reminder system for scheduling checkups and screening tests. And in general, physicians do not have easy access to protocols or best practices that are synchronized with an individual's health status. The best that many people can hope for is to receive a reminder card in the mail which they had self-addressed at their last checkup. And far too few humans are ever automatically reminded to have their cholesterol checked, their annual Pap smear done, or other routine screenings performed. When we consider how important prevention is and its powerful role in increasing longevity, it is inexcusable that our human healthcare system is so far behind the Lexus in this regard.

Japanese manufacturing: The whole becomes greater than the sum of its parts

Toyota, the parent company of Lexus, was one of several Japanese car manufacturing companies to revolutionize the automobile industry in the 1980s and early '90s. While Lexus stood out as a premium brand in its ability to use technology to deliver customized "care" and improve communication among Lexus technicians everywhere, the transformation of the automobile industry as a whole took place at two different levels. Before Japanese car companies could get to the level of customized services and satellite-linked information, they first had to step back and take a broad look at their design, manufacturing, and distribution processes and connect the disjointed elements so they could work as a complete, efficient system. The Japanese did not merely improve the speed of their assembly lines or throw more money at fixing the one piece of the manufacturing system that they perceived to be the weakest. Instead, they approached this challenge holistically and systematically. They made sure they saw the whole manufacturing, distribution, and customer service system from every angle so they could determine how each piece needed to work with the others to produce a distinctly higher-quality automobile at a notably lower cost than anything comparable in its class.

Japanese automakers used systems science to re-engineer their design, manufacturing, and distribution processes. Ironically, the principles they used were largely based on the work of W. Edwards Deming, an American who previously had been laughed out of Detroit. This disbelief in Deming's principles at the time warrants serious consideration in the context of this book. It simply did not make sense to U.S. auto companies that you could produce a substantially higher-quality product at a substantially lower cost. After all, Cadillacs and Lincolns were expensive cars with luxurious materials, and such luxury and comfort was viewed as having to cost more. Brand names commanded higher value; and as long as you could sell at a sufficiently high price, you could increase the expense to deliver the goods. And just imagine the gall of a self-proclaimed "efficiency expert" to tell Detroit automakers—who had created the largest product companies in the world—how to improve their businesses. Meanwhile, over in Europe, there was not only a strong emphasis on engineering superiority in automobile design, but also the general belief that such superiority should naturally cost more—in the case of Mercedes, much more.

In the early '80s we had dominant brands such as Chevrolet, Ford, and Chrysler producing automobiles with similar performance characteristics and selling them for prices that U.S. citizens had no choice but to accept. After all, people needed cars and that was what they cost. Just choose your model based upon your socioeconomic status. And of course, people got used to the price of a new model going up each year, along with the prices of gas, auto insurance, tires, and car repairs and maintenance. It was a seemingly perfect system and became the basis for entire regional economies. Consumers bought into the notion that in the category of automobiles, the price-performance curve was just the way things were meant to be. Does that behavior look familiar in the realm of U.S. healthcare?

You don't have to delve too deeply into the manufacturing processes of that time to know that the U.S. model of linear assembly lines, storing massive amounts of inventory, and performing quality checks late in the manufacturing process, after much of the work had been completed, was the antithesis of what Japanese automakers were cooking up. The Japanese took a page out of the European book on superiority of engineering design, adding their own knowledge of electronics. They worked in small teams, checking quality early and often to minimize re-work; they applied just-in-time concepts to avoid carrying expensive inventory; and they thought about how to extend their design and engineering specifications to distributors (auto dealers) for purposes of proactively maintaining the quality of their products even after they were delivered to consumers. As a result, Japanese automakers could design, build, and deliver automobiles faster and at a lower cost. Satisfaction among both customers and suppliers improved dramatically, and customer choice was enhanced by offering the consumer customization. Once U.S. consumers got over their disdain for unfamiliar brands (and the Japanese ultimately learned how to create brand appeal), Japanese automakers gained significant market share, because they were able to design much higher-quality cars more cost-effectively. And while I acknowledge competitive labor cost differences for U.S. automakers (in part because of the comparatively higher cost of U.S. healthcare), it is essential to understand that it was an overall change in systematic design on the part of the Japanese that set off the auto wars, with labor being one component of that system. In other words, the higher-quality-at-lower-cost curve demanded a new way—a better-engineered way—of process design.

Systematic thinking meets applied technology and information technology

Even if you are able to conceptualize a "better mousetrap" as Lexus did, it becomes an entirely different challenge to repeatedly produce high quality on a large scale. In other words, producing hundreds of thousands of automobiles and properly maintaining them, or managing tens of millions of healthcare consumers (patients) according to a series of best practices is a mind-boggling proposition. Fortunately, there are two types of technological advancements that help us humans accomplish things beyond our individual and collective capacity—applied technology and information technology.

It has often been said the definition of technology is anything that didn't exist when you were born. It's hilarious but true. My grandparents couldn't run their VCR, my parents can't run their home theater system, and I struggle to manipulate the touch screen on my kids' mobile audio devices. Each of these examples illustrates applied technology—how technology can be used in a specific industry or product group—in this case, media. In the automotive industry I just described, new types of sound-damping steel and aluminum alloys, robotics to repeat painting sequences with precision, and engineering design to shape a car to reduce its drag coefficient are all examples of *applied technologies*. In healthcare, examples of applied technologies are glucose meters for instantly measuring a diabetic's glucose level; the da Vinci® surgical robot that enables minimally invasive surgery; and, of course, biotechnological innovations that produce pharmaceutical chemical compounds and even stem cells that grow into replacement organs. Applied technology innovations are potentially infinite because they are ongoing. If you try to keep track of all of the applied technologies for an industry as vast as either manufacturing or healthcare, you would be hard-pressed to do so.

To take a systematic view, you have to accept the notion that as remarkable as these applied technology innovations are, they are just elements of the system and rarely provide the impetus for solving a total systems problem. For example, for 20 years I have listened to pundits explain how storing health records in a microchip embedded in an ID card is the panacea for healthcare, or that the digital mobile phone is the answer to the problem of delivering healthcare information to the right place at the right time. These prognostications are made by people I refer to as "gadget freaks" (who are usually in the business of selling gadgets). Doesn't it seem silly to consider carrying around a physical copy of your health records on a chip (which means your provider would have to have the gadget that can decode your chip) when secure Internet access is almost universally available? And as for the mobile phone, let's do a reality check on how many people can keep track of calls, voice messages, text messages, contacts, calendars, and MP3 music collections simultaneously before we assume that putting more information on the same gadget will not become merely another distraction. Nonetheless, applied technologies are often incredible, wonderful enablers of broader systematic designs.

Information technology is the second form of technology that helps humans systematically produce high quality on a scale as large as automobile manufacturing. Through information technology, the Japanese and ultimately U.S. automakers were able to link design, manufacturing, and distribution processes in a systematic way so that each element showed up when and where it should. A computer in and of itself is really just a gadget. But when you add software (instructions) and data, you are beginning to enter the realm of information technology. And when you apply computing, software, and data and information management to automate the work of people as well as processes and applied technology, you have stepped into the world of enterprise information technology. It is important to understand that without enterprise information technology, transformation of the auto industry would likely not have occurred. There would be no enterprises with the scale and efficiency of Walmart, and the United States would have no functioning private health insurance industry or a Medicare program serving millions of people.

During the late 1980s and into the 1990s, tremendous progress was made in the development of enterprise information technology solutions combining increasing computing power with complex software that could manipulate increasingly vast amounts of data. This progress continues today, and it's important to tie these innovations back to systematic thinking. The automotive industry first drove the innovation of what was originally called manufacturing requirements planning or MRP systems. These were software solutions where you enter a product design, keep track of all the materials and processes required to build it, track each piece and part through a series of automated and human labor processes, and keep track of the finished good. I had the chance to help develop and implement some of these early solutions, and it was a great background for thinking about the challenges in healthcare. Today, these early systems have evolved into what are known as enterprise resource planning or ERP systems, with such notable purveyors as Oracle and SAP. Similarly, early attempts at automated distribution systems to track demand by and facilitate sales to end-customers have developed into today's customer relationship management or CRM solutions. And enterprise information technology isn't just for manufacturers. Retail giant Walmart uses information technology linked from each of its check-out registers at each of its locations to each of its suppliers to optimize the availability and price of thousands of distributed products to meet the demand of millions of consumers.

Systems approach and the right technology can transform healthcare
So why have we not been able to make as significant inroads in solving the healthcare crisis as we have accomplished in the automotive, retail, and other industries? The information technology certainly exists to transform the healthcare system, but we first need to take a systematic approach to understanding and fixing the system. We are much like the automakers of the '80s in that we have some excellent processes that function as independent entities. Some of the linear "assembly lines" in doctors' offices, insurance companies, benefits administration companies, hospitals, disease management companies, the pharmaceutical industry, and in virtually every area of the healthcare system

are quite good at what they do. However, far too often each of these parts of the healthcare supply chain is like the blind men in the previous chapter—able to feel only its own part of the healthcare elephant and unable to see how the parts work together to form a complete system.

I am now on my second Lexus, after giving my first one—which is still in great health for its age—to my mother. Each time I take it in for maintenance and witness the efficiency of the Lexus service system, I am struck by the contrast between the quality practices for the care of the Lexus and those for the human. I don't mean to imply by my comparison that servicing cars and caring for human beings share the same level of complexity; obviously the latter is a far more nuanced endeavor. However, there is simply no reason, given the information technology that exists, that we can't engineer the healthcare system to give human beings care that is coordinated, consistent, efficient, and based on the best practices available today.

In Chapter Four we'll look at what composes the healthcare supply chain and how it is organized by both private payers and the federal and state governments. We'll also examine supply chains in the auto and retail industries and see how the organizers of all three supply chains attempt to balance supply and demand and add value to the system.

• • • • • • • • • • • • • •

Understanding the Healthcare Supply Chain

Chaos was the law of nature; Order was the dream of man.
— Henry Brooks Adams, American historian

Suppose you are the owner of the Lexus in the last chapter. How did you decide which type of car to purchase? Your decision may have been based on *Consumer Reports* ratings such as how many miles per gallon the car gets and the car's performance on safety measures. You probably also considered cost, appearance, ergonomics, how the car handles, its size relative to your hauling needs, and available color options. If you were very knowledgeable, you may have researched whether the car has a communications-linked system for repairs and maintenance, how quickly it loses its value after purchase, and its total cost of ownership over a five-year life or its average cost per mile, assuming you will drive it for 100,000 miles.

Behind the scenes: the supply chain

Once you decided on your Lexus, you probably compared prices from various dealerships and on-line sources before making your purchase. Although you may not have realized it at the time, when you bought your car you not only bought the vehicle but also the value added by the car's *supply chain*—the designers, producers, parts and labor suppliers, storage facilities, transporters, distributors, and network of retailers that participate in the sale, production and delivery of a particular product. In other words, from the time your car was designed, people and companies along the way provided their expertise in many areas, striving to enhance the value of the product so they would be paid proportionately for their contribution to its ultimate purchase price. They designed the car with an eye toward quality, style, and the outstanding service they know you deserve. In designing the car, they made sure recent technologies such as your daughter's MP3 player could plug into your car and play her favorite music and videos. They selected only the finest sound damping and non-corrosive metals for manufacturing and negotiated a reasonable purchase price for these materials. They assembled the car according to established production engineering guidelines to ensure consistency and quality and then they priced the car fairly while also eking out a profit. They established a network of dealerships where you could access the car for a test-drive and seek help from trained and knowledgeable sales staff, and they transported your car from the manufacturing plant to the dealership. They inspected the car, making sure it had all of the options you ordered and was clean and shiny, complete with a full tank of gas and even a fully charged hybrid battery when you closed the deal and drove it off the lot. They also reminded you about their communications-linked service system, bundled in your routine maintenance so that you would keep visiting Lexus dealerships even if you moved, and they offered you a discount on your first oil change. And they programmed all of the steps, from ordering your new car through production and delivery, into a computerized enterprise resource management system that could be accessed, updated and tracked by all participants in the supply chain to ensure quality and timeliness.

Of course, not all cars you test-drove impressed you quite like the one you selected. Maybe the price was too high for what you perceived the car was worth (possibly because the purchasers in that car's supply chain did not negotiate a good price for the materials they used). Or perhaps there were aspects of the design or quality that fell short. There are two points to be made about how you decided which car to buy and how this decision relates to healthcare:

First, each product or service you purchase has its own supply chain, which affects how you perceive its value—the level of quality you get for the price you pay.

Second, if you are not able to evaluate certain information to determine value when making a purchase, it is very difficult to match expectations to results. I have learned that most people determine value based upon whether a good or service meets or exceeds their expectation for the price they paid.

In the U.S. healthcare system, the ability of a typical consumer—you or me—to assess the value of services rendered is generally accepted to be something of an enigma. This is the case for a number of reasons, not the least of which is that, historically, consumers have not known the total cost of the healthcare services they receive. For example, do you know whether a prescription drug you pick up at the pharmacy for $10 has a retail price of $439, or perhaps even $4.99? We have gotten used to this phenomenon in healthcare, so it may seem perfectly normal; however, can you imagine a world where having automobile insurance entitles you to use a car, anytime you want, for a $5 co-pay? Not just when your car is in the shop, but every day? We will explore this issue later in the book, but it's important for any consumer to step back and systematically consider the elements of supply chain and value. Of course, this is best done when you are not in dire need of medical care, as it is a very rare person who can make value-based inquiries of his doctor or other members of the medical staff when lying unclothed under a paper gown, facing the anxiety of his own health challenges. Over the years, I have evolved into just such a creature, a fact my doctors tend to find entertaining. However, my hope is that as you read this book, you are in a more comfortable setting to think holistically about the supply chain and to see the clear health and cost benefits of creating a truly integrated healthcare supply chain.

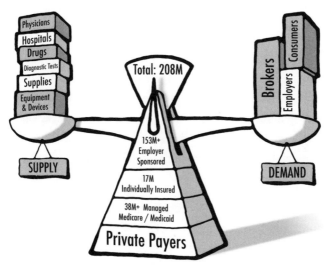

Elements of the healthcare supply chain
There are many types of *suppliers* as well as *providers*, ranging from medical doctors, behavioral health professionals, dentists, and social workers to alternative and integrated medicine practitioners, any of whom may operate

in business models ranging from individual to institutional. In an organized system of healthcare, the bulk of the supply chain consists of several elements on the supply side:

Doctors are the most obvious providers because they are the people with whom you have the most contact when you need care. Their role in the supply chain is to provide hands-on medical care and health information to patients. They also order diagnostic tests and procedures they deem necessary in order to evaluate a patient's condition. Primary care doctors in internal medicine, family practice, pediatrics, and increasingly obstetrics-gynecology (Ob-Gyn) and gerontology manage the overall health of their patients and evaluate whether patients need to see a specialist or take medication to control a particular condition. As we'll discuss further in Chapter Eight, many types of specialty physicians are increasingly assuming the role of primary care physician under a model known as the patient-centered medical home. *Primary care doctors* are often aided by physician assistants or nurse practitioners who are also highly trained and help manage the patient load. *Specialists* such as orthopedists, neurologists, oncologists or podiatrists have additional medical training focusing on a specific part of the anatomy, a particular illness, or care related to a certain population group. Doctors can practice alone, in groups with similar types of doctors, or in multi-specialty clinics where primary care doctors and specialists work side by side. Other licensed healthcare professionals, including nurses and physical therapists, also work with primary care doctors and specialists to provide care. *Nurses* are essential to the process of caring for patients and, although they generally prepare patients for exams and carry out physicians' orders, they are the human thread that stitches together the total patient experience. And much like primary care physicians, nurses are in short supply for the near and long term.

Hospitals are another type of care provider that offers specialized facilities and infrastructure along with medical expertise. In addition to emergency room doctors there are physicians, known as *hospitalists*, who practice primarily on-site at hospitals; doctors who specialize in certain diseases (e.g., oncologists) and organs (e.g., cardiologists); and of course nurses and medical technicians. The medical staff at hospitals provides emergency, surgical, inpatient, outpatient (sometimes called ambulatory) and other care typically not available at your doctor's office and treats patients in very serious situations for which a primary care doctor might not have the necessary expertise, equipment or environment (such as an operating room). Most people don't realize that the majority of doctors in hospitals (besides ER doctors and hospitalists) are not there all the time, but rather run practices, admit patients, perform procedures and do "rounds" where they check in on their patients. Many hospitals have specialized units or *centers of excellence* staffed by highly trained specialists who perform complex procedures such as heart or lung transplants or brain surgery. Other hospitals may specialize in treating burn victims, spinal injuries, or patients with cancer. Still others are known as *skilled nursing facilities* where patients may complete their recovery. Hospitals, whether general or dedicated to a particular specialty, provide concentrated expertise combined with the equipment, supplies and environment necessary to treat serious illnesses and conditions. Quite often, general hospitals in highly populated areas also have clinics distributed around the flagship hospital to extend their expertise into the communities they serve. These clinics usually perform only outpatient procedures and tests.

Diagnostic centers are another type of care provider that most healthcare consumers encounter. These include medical labs, imaging centers (where you receive X-rays, magnetic resonance imaging (MRI), and other advanced types of radiological imaging), and a variety of centers that specialize in such things as cardiac, pulmonary, and gastroenterological (digestive tract) testing. Although the results from these tests may be reviewed by highly specialized physicians (e.g., radiologists) and technicians, they typically are passed directly to the physician who ordered them.

Pharmacies fill prescriptions written by doctors and other authorized healthcare professionals and check to see whether the medication prescribed is covered by the patient's health plan so they can determine what the consumer owes versus and what to bill to the health plan. They also add value by alerting patients to possible drug interactions and explaining exactly how and when to take various medications. Some pharmacists make recommendations of over-the-counter remedies for patients who don't feel sick enough to go to the doctor. In addition, pharmacy benefit managers, who work for the pharmacy, independently, or for various health plans, establish formularies, check whether patients are covered for certain medications, and determine when generic drugs may be substituted.

Vendors of medical equipment, devices and supplies sell or rent items such as oxygen transport systems, glucose meters, blood pressure cuffs, crutches, canes, back braces, wheelchairs, home intravenous drug infusion systems, and other tangible items used directly by healthcare consumers. Items that can be reused by multiple patients are often referred to as durable medical equipment. There are also disposable supplies for eye care, wound care, incontinence management, ostomy management, and many other medical conditions. These supplies are usually expensive and may not be available in your corner drug store, but are used and disposed of on a regular basis by many healthcare consumers. Systematically, you probably realize that there are device and equipment manufacturers that sell only to hospitals, doctors, clinics and diagnostic centers. They sell single-use items such as drug-eluting stents and pacemakers as well as imaging machines, dialysis machines, electronic patient monitoring stations, and other expensive capital items that a consumer, unless endowed with a fortune, would not typically purchase for personal use. Also, as I mentioned earlier, pharmaceutical companies that develop drugs and other biotechnology entities supply an array of goods in bulk to pharmacies and hospitals (as well as samples to doctors). The process of developing these applied technologies is costly, and the high price of these products often reflects the manufacturer's need to recoup development costs. Not all equipment and supply companies provide the same level of quality or charge the same amount for their goods. Because the typical consumer lacks expertise in this area, it is the job of the organizer of the supply chain to select companies and products that offer high quality at the best price.

There are also several elements on the demand side of the healthcare supply chain:

Employers, as they relate to the healthcare supply chain, are "aggregators" of healthcare consumers. In other words, they provide an entry point for consumers into the healthcare supply chain through financial arrangements they make with the health plans they offer to employees. Many people may not realize the value added by employers, who often pay a large percentage of the total healthcare premium cost for their employees. For the most part, whether or not an employer offers health benefits depends on its size and financial status. For example, some small employers offer only very basic coverage with high out-of-pocket costs for their employees, or they do not offer health insurance at all. On the other hand, many larger employers go beyond basic health insurance to offer wellness and disease management programs that help employees stay healthy and manage chronic illnesses, such as diabetes. The role of the employer will be discussed in the next chapter, but it should be understood that in the United States, it is almost a given that employers are directly involved in the healthcare supply chain to make sure their employees have access to health insurance coverage. In many other countries, this is absolutely not the case.

Brokers play an important role in helping consumers and employers decide which health plan company and what types of benefits will best meet their respective needs. Brokers help organize the demand side of the supply chain. Today, depending on market segment, between 75 percent and 100 percent of all health insurance is purchased through over one million[8] licensed life and health brokers across the United States. Brokers are perceived as advocates for purchasers of all types, including senior citizens, self-employed individuals, small and mid-sized employer groups, and large multi-state employers. Brokers who primarily distribute group benefits typically have a direct relationship with employers. Most people who receive insurance benefits through their employers (i.e., over 150 million of us) do not know that brokers are the primary drivers of our companies' benefit choices. Within the past few years, rising healthcare costs and increased benefit design complexity have created more opportunity for brokers to differentiate their services. Their responsibilities historically have included purchasing guidance, enrollment assistance, billing and claims status inquiries, and policy renewals, though some brokers now include administration of wellness and other preventive health programs in their spectrum of services.

Consumers are people like you and me. We require different amounts and types of healthcare depending on our age, health status, financial situation and values, thus filling out the demand side of the supply chain. However, although there generally is a predictable pattern as we move from birth to our senior years, as the Healthcare Life Stage chart shows, one single event such as an accident or an acute or chronic illness can instantly change a person's health status and income.

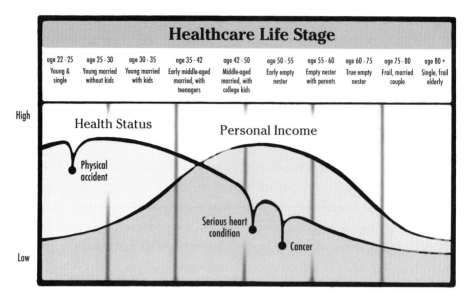

Healthcare Life Stage									
age 22 - 25	age 25 - 30	age 30 - 35	age 35 - 42	age 42 - 50	age 50 - 55	age 55 - 60	age 60 - 75	age 75 - 80	age 80 +
Young & single	Young married without kids	Young married with kids	Early middle-aged married, with teenagers	Middle-aged married, with college kids	Early empty nester	Empty nester with parents	True empty nester	Frail, married couple	Single, frail elderly

Source: Thomas J. Main, partner and U.S. market leader, Oliver Wyman Health and Life Sciences

In the middle of the supply chain are **payers**, commonly known as **health plans**, organizing systems of benefits and care to balance supply and demand within an economic set of constraints (i.e., at an affordable price). As the previous supply chain illustration shows, private payers – known to most consumers as insurance companies such as BlueCross BlueShield affiliates, Aetna, CIGNA, United Health Group and Humana – carry out this function. Public payers, such as the federal and state governments oversee Medicare, Medicaid, and several other programs, but as we will see, they do not typically organize benefits and care in the same manner as private plans.

There are also many other elements of the supply chain that are a step or more removed from the consumer, such as pharmaceutical companies that sell supplies to pharmacies. As well, there are many federal and state regulatory bodies that have an impact on virtually every element of the supply chain. I will touch on only a few examples of these types of value chain participants in order to promote your understanding, as the purpose of this book is to be systematic, but not exhaustive.

The Yellow Pages approach to getting care

Given all the elements of the healthcare supply chain, imagine a world where it's completely up to you to organize them. In the most extreme cases, you might find yourself flipping through the *Yellow Pages* or surfing the Internet to find a doctor. If you look under "physicians," there is a very lengthy list. Where would you start? If your foot hurt, would you go to an orthopedist, an internist, a nephrologist, or a podiatrist? Assuming you were able to direct yourself to the correct specialty, how would you know which doctor to choose? Would you select a doctor based on cost, on whether someone you know has seen him, or on where he went to medical school? Further adding to your confusion is the fact that you have no idea what services you need, so you cannot possibly know how much your appointment will cost. In short, you are stuck in the middle of a very complex non-system with no information on quality or cost and no one to help you down the path that makes the most sense for you. Can you organize your own supply chain of doctors, hospitals (in the event you need surgery for your foot), pharmacies, diagnostic testing services, and medical supplies that will ensure that you receive high-quality care at a predetermined price? Or are you truly in the heart of the healthcare jungle?

Balancing supply and demand: organizers of the healthcare supply chain

Now that we have looked at the parts of the healthcare supply chain, let's further examine who organizes it. In order for any supply chain to exist, someone has to develop business arrangements with suppliers or vendors who meet a set of quality, cost and service standards. In the case of Lexus, the supply chain is organized by Toyota, which negotiates contracts with certain vendors that have met its requirements. These contracts and the complex negotiations that precede them are invisible to you if you purchase a Lexus, but they are a critical part of its creation. Similarly, you do not see the technology that enables service information to be accessed by all Lexus service departments; however, without it, you would not receive the comprehensive, coordinated service you have come to expect.

In healthcare, the organizers of the supply chain are private payers as well as the federal government and individual state governments in the role of payers. These entities bring together certain providers and vendors into a network that can give you healthcare at a price within your means and that is accessible to you either directly (through an individual or "self-pay" plan) or through your employer.

Private payers, such as health plans, provide medical and specialty coverage for more than 200 million people in the United States. Approximately 700 private payers negotiate competitive pricing arrangements with doctors, hospitals, diagnostic companies, pharmacy benefit managers and vendors of supplies and equipment, and bundle this vast array of complex services into benefit plans that meet the needs of employers and individuals. Payers sell their benefit plans to the person in charge of benefits (often the human resource department) at the employer as well as to people seeking coverage on their own (either directly or through a broker), enabling consumers to enroll in the plans and access the doctors, hospitals and care facilities that compose their "delivery network." Payers also make this coverage available for a period of time (through the COBRA program) to people who had been covered under their employer's health coverage but who no longer receive health benefits through an employer group. Payers provide service to consumers, providers, pharmacists, employers and brokers by answering questions about what services are covered for consumers in their benefit plans. In addition, payers manage contracts and relationships with all parts of the supply chain, keep track of premium payments made by employers (or individuals), process claims based on negotiated prices, and determine who is responsible for paying which portion of the costs. Historically, payers have played a transaction-oriented role in the supply chain, processing claims that come in and authorizing payment for covered services. Depending upon the type of benefit plan, payers also get involved to various degrees in driving efficient use of healthcare resources, ensuring consumers are getting appropriate care from appropriate providers, and proactively helping consumers pursue better health and wellness. (Note: Payers that take on financial risk are also regarded as "health insurers," whereas payers that organize the system of benefits and care and then process transactions for self-funded employer groups are regarded as third-party administrators [TPAs] or administrative-services-only providers [ASOs]. Health plans typically offer employers a choice of insured or self-funded products, and are capable of administering both.)

Public payers, such as federal and state governments also organize supply chains for health coverage for about 100 million people in the United States, approximately one-third of whom choose to assign their benefit coverage to private health plans through such programs as Medicare Advantage and managed Medicaid. The government establishes benefit packages for various segments of our society for whom it is responsible by law, determines who will be eligible for each plan, negotiates pricing arrangements with certain providers and hospitals, and manages (or contracts with a private payer to manage) the claims and other financial operations. See the benefits plan chart that follows for more detail on health coverage plans organized by the state and federal governments.

Major Government-Organized Health Benefit Plans

Product	Who it is for	Supply Chain Organizer	Approximate Number of Beneficiaries
Medicare	• people age 65 and over • people under age 65 with certain disabilities, and • people of all ages with End-Stage Renal Disease	federal government via the Centers for Medicare and Medicaid Services (CMS)	45.3 million (as of 7/1/08—includes approximately 7.7M disabled)
Medicaid	primarily for people with very low income levels	state governments, with assistance and oversight from CMS	46.6 million (12/31/08 estimate)
TRICARE	active-duty military personnel and their families	federal government (Department of Defense)	1.4 million
Department of Veterans Affairs	honorably discharged veterans and their dependents	federal government (Department of Veterans Affairs)	8.0 million
Federal Employee Health Benefits Program	employees of the federal government and their families	federal government, which in most cases, contracts with private payers to supply the benefits administration	8.0 million

Organized systems of payment and delivery versus
organized systems of benefits and care

Everywhere you turn you hear that the U.S. healthcare system (the supply chain of healthcare) delivers too little quality for too much cost. But what does this really mean? Quite simply, the total cost of healthcare for either an individual or a population of patients equals the price that is paid for each unit of care received (such as an office visit, a prescription or a hospital stay) times the number of occurrences of each of those units.

$$\text{Total cost of healthcare} = \text{Unit cost} \times \text{Number of units}$$

Therefore, in order to deliver higher-quality healthcare for fewer dollars, we need to systematically manage 1) the unit price element, 2) the number of units, and 3) the effectiveness or outcome of the results produced by those units.

How do we achieve this ambitious goal of delivering units of quality care at an affordable price? In the United States, two models organized around providers have emerged: the organized system of payment and the integrated delivery system.

Historically, government-organized supply chains for Medicare and state Medicaid programs essentially have been *organized systems of payment*. This means that while the government establishes (or imposes) pricing with its providers and suppliers regarding reimbursement for care delivery, this care is not systematically organized or coordinated in any substantial way and there is typically no relationship among the primary care doctors, specialists, imaging centers, pharmacies, hospitals, and other parts of the supply chain, apart from the fact that they all have pricing contracts with the government. With a few exceptions, our government primarily serves as an organizer of payments, not an organizer of the entire healthcare supply chain.

In *integrated delivery systems*, one or more hospitals along with other affiliated components of the supply side of the supply chain (e.g., physicians and diagnostic centers, etc.) strive to share information, minimize duplication and make treatment decisions based upon the institutional best practices for the patient's given situation. An example of a governmental integrated delivery system is run by the Department of Veterans Affairs (the "VA"), which offers military personnel care through an integrated system of government-owned (and privately sub-contracted) hospitals and clinics, along with dedicated health professionals. It should be noted here that there is a certain elegant simplicity to the electronic sharing of information (i.e., electronic health records) about VA beneficiaries (veterans who are patients), as they receive the majority of their care at VA facilities that all run on common systems, and patients stay in the system for their entire lives (in contrast to most U.S. citizens who change health plans multiple times). The VA is a glimpse of what a "single payer" system—where the benefits and providers are under centralized control—looks like.

It is important systematically to note that both TRICARE (the health program for active military) and the VA (for retired military) follow the pattern of centralized control for the U.S defense system, and like that system, is funded through taxation. Examples like the VA, where there is a benefit plan that lines up directly with an integrated delivery system, also exist in the private sector. One of the better-known is Kaiser Permanente, where primary care, specialty care, diagnostic testing, and even pharmacies are located at company-run health centers. Within integrated delivery networks like these, the best chance exists to coordinate units of care effectively under the control of providers. However, although care may be well *coordinated* in these settings the *efficiency* of that care is questionable when you take a systems science view. For example, when I was an executive with an integrated delivery system that owned hospitals, physician groups, pharmacies and diagnostic centers there was always a lot of pressure to keep the beds filled and the equipment humming for the sake of "full utilization leading to efficiency."

But truly integrated delivery systems are rare in both the public and private sectors, as they require tremendous amounts of both financial and political capital to link facilities with physicians. In the private sector, they typically are organized in urban or high-density suburban areas containing one or more leading hospitals. Nearby private physician practices, and often physicians with academic relationships to local universities, set up localized delivery systems that include hospitals, specialists, and primary care doctors. Although these entities might not all be located in the same building, they work with one another in a systematic, coordinated way, giving patients the impression of having all services under one roof. And keep in mind that for most local "health systems" (the name often given to integrated delivery systems), there is no direct linkage between consumers' benefit plans and the care they receive. In other words, the integrated delivery system is just operating on the supply side of the supply chain. Compare this to the VA, Kaiser and a handful of other integrated delivery systems, where the payer has direct control over facilities and providers.

Although we've discussed the relative advantages of coordinating care in integrated delivery systems, in the majority of large American cities and certainly in suburban and rural settings, the delivery of care to you as a consumer is more typically fragmented. This is due to a combination of factors, including consumer desire for choice, and provider competition (multiple hospitals, independent physicians, different pharmacy chains, etc.) . For example, a painkiller prescribed by a specialist may never make it into the medical records kept by the primary care doctor who saw you initially for the same illness or injury (episode of care). Similarly, test results are not systematically sent from one doctor to another, often resulting in repetition of the same test by multiple physicians. Even referrals from primary care doctors to specialists are based largely on which specialist a given primary care doctor knows—not on who objectively would be the best specialist to perform a particular procedure, or even who has the most competitive pricing. Without an organized delivery system that is tied into a benefit plan, there is no systematic way to predict costs, encourage high-quality delivery of care, or minimize overlap. As a result, it is up to the individual patient or doctor to push through the healthcare jungle and try to create order out of the chaos. When care and payments are truly coordinated, it's almost accidental. Wouldn't it be better to make it systematic?

Organized payment and integrated delivery are good, but fall short
My point, and the point of this book, is that neither an organized system of payment nor an integrated delivery system approach is optimal. The right application of technology and processes affords us a way to make the coordinated delivery of benefits and care possible anywhere in the country. Moreover, I believe (and studies support) that moving to this approach—which I call Integrated Healthcare Management—can knock 20 percent to 30 percent off the total amount we are spending on healthcare while improving the quality of outcomes. More on this later, but first, let's further understand systematic examples from other industries.

The supply chains of "big-box" retail stores and their virtual cousins
In order to better understand the value of a fully functioning supply chain, let's take a trip to our local Walmart. Walmart takes a set of demands from its customers, such as the need for reasonably priced hygiene items or photography products and services, and organizes a set of suppliers and service providers to meet these needs. Walmart also carefully manages this supply chain and makes adjustments as it learns more about its customers' needs and preferences. It monitors demand for certain items on a real-time basis. If it sees demand increase for a particular item, it orders more of that item from its supplier. And if Walmart notices certain products being returned over and over, Walmart either discusses the problem with its supplier or stops carrying these items. Walmart continually and systematically monitors its inventory, the performance of its suppliers, and the demands of its consumers in order to make sure the supply meets the consumers' demand for the highest-quality products at the lowest prices. These systematic principles of effective price negotiation, efficient distribution, constant monitoring of customer preferences and strict attention to quality enable Walmart to do well both when the overall economy is doing well and during periods of economic challenge.

Amazon (i.e., Amazon.com) is an example of another well-designed system of logistics and supply-chain management that is virtual (i.e., non-physical). Although you can't walk the aisles of an Amazon store, its offers and prices are clearly communicated to the prospective purchaser in an on-line encounter. Importantly, consumers have a sense of exactly what they are getting for a certain price and when it will arrive. In addition, the consumer can view the product and read reviews from others who have previously experienced it. This example exists in stark contrast to the current state of healthcare purchasing, where consumers stand mired in the jungle without a clear sense of what is being delivered, what that delivery will cost, and what is its ultimate value. As with Walmart, the Amazon experience did not evolve randomly as a result of multiple suppliers interacting under their traditional models, but rather, was designed and engineered by Amazon (using the best of conventional physical supply-chain management) with the virtual consumer in mind.

The approach of Amazon has been telling. Consumers have signaled their strong approval of the Amazon model, increasing their on-line buying at the expense of traditional brick-and-mortar establishments. Amazon also has pioneered reliable delivery of products that used to be exclusively physical (e.g., books) into electronic form, such as book delivery via an electronic reading device. This has occurred even amid economic uncertainty, showing that when consumers are exposed to a clearly communicated value proposition that delivers value to them in a more convenient way they tend to embrace it.

So what does Walmart or Amazon have to do with the United States healthcare system? Obviously, healthcare is much more complex than a big-box chain store. After all, retail stores primarily provide products you can touch, feel or see, while healthcare is focused on a very specialized set of services. However, just as we explored the successes of the manufacturer of the Lexus in Chapter Three, there is much we can learn from the systematic way in which stores like Walmart organize and manage their supply chains. Every Walmart store throughout the country has an organized supply chain with pre-negotiated pricing. In addition, the pricing is clearly communicated and payment is understood and collected at the moment you go through checkout (at the point of service). Amazon does the same thing during on-line checkout. In other words, the pricing is visible and transparent to everyone from the consumer to the company's chief financial officer to the cashier ringing up the sale.

Healthcare lacks transparency for consumers and providers
In contrast to retail, pricing in healthcare is rarely fully understood by the consumer or doctor's office. Although in many cases the healthcare supply chain organizers have negotiated pricing and discounts with providers and suppliers, that pricing is not transparent or clearly communicated to patients and providers. Do we know how much of our premium is used to pay for medical expenses or to protect us from spending all of our savings should a medical catastrophe occur (the insurance portion of our premium)? We simply pay what we are asked to pay and assume we'll be covered for whatever we need. And rarely do we know in advance of a procedure or appointment what the real cost of these services is. This approach would never work in retail and it is one of the reasons our healthcare system is in such dire financial straits. That is, with an absence of pricing information, it is difficult (if not impossible) for a consumer to determine value. And if consumers do not make healthcare choices based on value, then our healthcare system cannot become more efficient.

In addition to the pricing differences between retail chains and the healthcare delivery system, there is another important difference between retail and healthcare. Retail stores like Walmart offer all their products under one roof—or in the case of Amazon—virtually, on one site.

This one-stop shopping approach enables the consumer to buy many different items—from beverages and candy to tablecloths and candles—all at the same place. In contrast, the healthcare delivery system is most often spread over a number of different physical locations. For example, if you go to your primary care doctor for a checkup you will often need to make a separate stop at a lab for blood work. Similarly, if you have a knee problem, you might go from your primary care doctor to a specialist's office and sometimes to a separate location for diagnostic tests. If you need to see the physical therapist or to have surgery you probably have to make additional trips. Each of these stops creates additional complexity for consumers and providers alike. The physical separation of many providers from one another is even more reason for our healthcare system to apply the fundamental principles of the retail world in order to develop a more seamless, coordinated system. It may seem pejorative to regard physicians, who are highly educated and make life-and-death decisions, as suppliers to be organized in a supply chain. But from a systems science perspective, that is the case. There are numerous other examples of life-and-death suppliers in other supply chains, from the seemingly simple engineering and manufacturing of a seat belt to the complex construction of bridges and jet airliners.

Private payers' attempts to systematize healthcare

Over the past several decades, healthcare experts in the United States have experimented with various ways to rein in costs and improve the quality of our healthcare supply chain in a systematic way. We started with basic health insurance in the 1950s when actuaries tried to predict, based on past experience with similar groups of people, how much care would be used for a given population. The actuaries then set a price for the insurance premium based on how much care they thought this group of people would receive over a set period of time. During some years, people used more care than predicted and in other years they used less. The challenge was to accurately predict the utilization so the insurance company could set a price that would cover the cost of care. Health insurance that predicts but does not manage risk, however, has very little to do with an organized supply chain, and after a while people realized this approach missed the mark.

In the 1980s, the concept of "managed care" began to evolve. As its name suggests, managed care marked the beginning of a more systematic approach to healthcare, where instead of predicting or guessing how much care people would use, HMOs set up organized networks of doctors, hospitals, pharmacies, and vendors of equipment and medical supplies. Pricing was negotiated in advance with each of the elements of what became the healthcare supply chain. The "maintenance" in health maintenance organization was similar to the Lexus service approach in Chapter Three: If you have preventive checkups and screenings at regular intervals and according to established guidelines, you may be more likely to stay healthy and less likely to need a big repair. HMOs introduced the primary care doctor as one who would take care of you as a whole person—not just as a broken ankle or a case of pneumonia. Through routine screenings, patient education, smoking cessation programs, parenting programs, and other initiatives considered innovative at the time, your HMO would not only treat you when you were sick but also try to help you stay well. Best of all, your primary care doctor could help you find the right in-network specialist to treat the pain in your foot so you would not be stuck leafing through the phone book for a doctor or trying to build your own supply chain.

Going from health insurance to health maintenance meant shifting from a reactive mode to one with more deliberate control over care and costs. If healthcare was heading in a more systematic direction then why did this fine nation not embrace the HMO model as its official system? The simple answer is limits. (The more complex answer is the political expediency of criticizing those limits when they were misapplied.) In order for HMOs to manage care and costs effectively, they have to set rules for when patients can receive certain types of care and from whom they can receive it. So in addition to their roles as healers and promoters of health, primary care doctors must determine when it is "medically necessary" for patients to see specialists, undergo tests or get access to complex or even experimental treatments. For example, it is reasonable to assume that if a patient sees a doctor for a mole on her back, the doctor will remove it if it meets the guidelines for removal; however, if it does not appear to be dangerous, the doctor might ask the patient to return at regular intervals to have the growth checked. The patient can always choose to have the growth removed, but if removal is not judged by the primary care doctor to be medically necessary, the patient must pay out-of-pocket for the care associated with removing the mole.

Another example has to do with the concept of self-referral to specialists. Let's go back to the example in Chapter Two of a hurt elbow from a tennis game. If you started your journey by going directly to the office of an orthopedic sur-geon, the likelihood of having an imaging test or a minimally invasive surgical procedure known as arthroscopy would increase, because the orthopedic spe-cialist is trained to diagnose and treat in a particular way. While the orthopedist is just trying in earnest to solve the patient's problem, both test and procedure are expensive, and one risks complications. Perhaps a visit or discussion with a primary care physician or access to self-care information would reduce the number of unnecessary tests.

In conventional managed care, there are also examples where testing or proce-dures that do, in fact, make good medical sense are either denied or the barriers to obtaining them are too high. This is not good, either. The biggest challenge for managed care organizations such as HMOs and for our healthcare system in general is to help consumers understand that in order to control costs and improve quality we need an organized system of benefits and care, but that all organized systems rely on rules, limits and informed decisions regarding value and effectiveness in order to help keep costs down and quality up.

Health plans have broad perspective to lead change
The United States is at a critical juncture for healthcare. As more people live longer and our population increases, our overall health status as a nation is declining, and the total demand for healthcare services will continue to rise. Put simply, more people are in need of more care, which means more money will be spent on healthcare unless we find a systematic way to provide this care more efficiently and help people be as healthy as possible. There are ongoing policy debates in Washington about how much money should be raised and how it should be distributed, from a payment perspective, across the healthcare supply chain. However, agreeing on an exact dollar amount to be allotted for each component in healthcare is far less important than designing our system to work more efficiently than it does today. We need to figure out how to do more for less under any circumstance. But who has a broad view of all of the

elements of the healthcare system in order to be able to make it function more efficiently? I contend that private health plans, like the ones running today's managed care programs, are best positioned (despite current shortcomings) to show leadership in systematically engineering the U.S. healthcare system, because they already sit at the center of the healthcare supply chain. In this capacity, they manage large groups of people and they have significant investments and experience in underlying information technology infrastructure as a baseline from which to improve. To give you some perspective on the scale of these private enterprises, the biggest private payers in the United States manage larger populations than the populations of entire countries such as the Netherlands, Sweden, and even Canada, to which our own healthcare system is compared. Private payers negotiate contracts, assemble the value-added components of the supply chain, and are at the heart of interactions with all of the supply chain elements. Like the wise man in the parable in Chapter Two, payers can best touch all of the parts of the system already and are in the best position to see the system as a whole. Consequently, most private payers fully understand that organized systems of payment are insufficient. And while there is recognition that integrated delivery system models can be very effective where available, new types of partnerships linking benefits and care must be forged by payers among all types of providers on behalf of consumers.

In order to fix a broken system, whether it is in manufacturing, mail delivery, or healthcare, one of the first steps is to look closely at the needs of the constituents or "players" in the system. In Chapter Five we will examine what consumers, providers, employers and brokers need from the healthcare system and how those needs are changing.

●●●●●●●●●●●●●●

The Perspectives of Healthcare Constituents

What you see and hear depends a good deal on where you are standing.
– C.S. Lewis, 'The Magician's Nephew'

In Chapter Four, we saw that few truly integrated delivery systems exist in this country and that most care is fragmented, with little coordination among the parts of the system. And as we saw in Chapter Two, some of the parts of the system do not even know the others exist, let alone understand how they work. Classic systems-design techniques suggest that we must consider the interplay of people, processes and technology in order to properly understand and design systematic solutions. In the case of the healthcare system, the constituents are the people who consume, provide, finance, distribute and manage healthcare products and services. Designing an integrated, coordinated healthcare system where all of the parts interact smoothly and efficiently requires us to step into the shoes of each of the healthcare constituents—consumers, providers, employers, brokers, and health plans. What are their respective roles, responsibilities and incentives? How does the system need to work for them? Are they getting what they need? How does one constituent's needs affect the others? The chart that follows below summarizes the *lifecycle* of the constituents and their respective experiences with the healthcare system over the course of a typical year. Only by understanding these lifecycles and the interactions constituents have with one another can we begin to design a healthcare system that works for everyone. Let's begin by looking at these interactions through the eyes of the consumer.

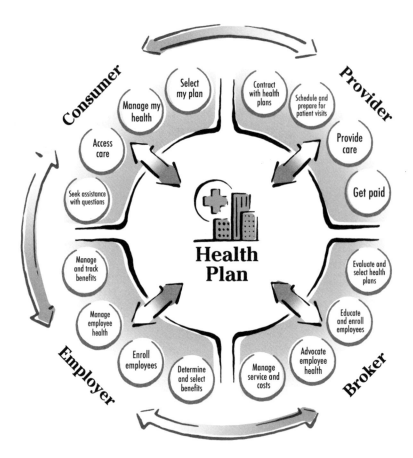

Consumers' expanding role in healthcare decision-making

As consumers we are in the midst of an ever-changing healthcare jungle. Until recently, we paid little of the healthcare premium and enjoyed health benefits with low out-of-pocket costs. As a result, many of us have long thought of health benefits as an entitlement. But now, as healthcare inflation outstrips growth in GDP, employers are being forced to share more of the cost of healthcare coverage with their employees, reduce benefits, or eliminate coverage entirely. This affordability crisis is forcing many consumers to take greater responsibility for their healthcare decisions, including a larger stake in the financial implications of their decisions. People don't necessarily want greater responsibility. I often say that consumers did not ask for consumer-directed healthcare; however, economic realities are driving change. And yet, for many families the total amount paid for health insurance premiums, deductibles and co-insurance ends up being one of their largest household expenditures each year.

As our responsibility for making informed healthcare decisions increases, the existing system is poorly equipped to help us in our new role. In addition, the healthcare system does not always provide incentives for behaviors and choices that will lead to better health and better outcomes. Few resources are spent on addressing our emerging needs: selecting coverage that is appropriate for our family's economic, life-stage and health status; planning for anticipated short- and long-term costs; evaluating resources to keep us healthy; and ultimately getting assistance in effectively navigating the care setting when we need to use it.

The consumer lifecycle can be broken into four significant steps: *selecting a plan, managing one's health, accessing care, and seeking assistance with questions.* Let's discuss each of these briefly.

1. Selecting a plan. Choosing health coverage may be one of the most important decisions you make each year. The plan you choose determines what care is covered, which doctors, hospitals and pharmacies are in your network and how much you will pay when you receive care. Health benefits are becoming increasingly complex and contain many trade-offs among cost, choice and coverage. As personal financial responsibility increases, how you save and pay for both short- and long-term healthcare costs becomes as important as the doctor or coverage you choose. Consumers need tools and information for selecting health plans and determining the best way to anticipate and pay for the care they will use. However the little information that is available is often on paper, or in formats that make comparison difficult. Today, many of us feel we must make our "best guess" among our alternatives, and hope that things work out.

Selecting and enrolling in a health plan is a multi-step process and varies slightly based on whether your coverage is employer-sponsored, purchased directly from your health plan, or arranged through a government-sponsored plan such as Medicare or Medicaid. If you get your health insurance through an employer, the employer generally provides education regarding benefit options and cost trade-offs. If you purchase health insurance directly, your health plan or broker provides that information. To help navigate the enormous volume of information about health coverage options, employers and health plans might provide on-line tools to guide you in making decisions. Some might even offer you the ability to enroll on-line in the plan of your choice, without your having to deal with cumbersome forms. Once you enroll, your health plan typically sends you an ID card, which signals that you are officially eligible to receive care.

2. Staying healthy. Staying healthy has different meanings depending upon your health status. If you are generally healthy, it is about prevention and being able to make good healthcare decisions regarding exercise, nutrition, and other daily activities that keep you out of the doctor's office. A rapidly increasing number of Americans are at risk for illnesses such as diabetes or heart disease. For them, staying healthy might mean following the doctor's recommended changes to diet and exercise as well as regularly taking prescribed medications to help delay or prevent the onset of disease. For people who have developed disease, staying healthy means doing the best they can to slow the progression of (or even reverse) the condition they have developed. The fact is that we as consumers perform most of the activities related to staying well (roughly 80 percent) right in the comfort of our own homes.[9]

To help you stay healthy, you need effective on-line tools, services and infor-mation about key aspects of your health. Consumers (and their doctors) are increasingly turning to social networks like Twitter and Facebook to connect in real time about specific health issues or about more general healthcare topics. Blogs (Web logs) also provide a forum for more in-depth discussion on health topics and can help to answer patient questions not answered during a time-pressured doctor visit. With these types of social media, more people than ever before can educate themselves about health topics.

However, we receive virtually no systematic guidance from the healthcare system and it is up to each of us to research and make sense of the overwhelming amount of information on the Internet and from well-meaning friends and relatives. Once you are enrolled in a health plan, today's system largely ignores you until you eventually do seek care, triggering a chain of financial and administrative tasks, such as claims and customer service inquiries, that historically have been the focus of health plans. However, there is growing attention and effort being focused on determining how health plans and providers can become more effective "partners in health" with their members and patients. In keeping with the old adage "an ounce of prevention is worth a pound of cure," many employers and health plans are zeroing in on wellness and prevention, as well as chronic disease management, as methods to reduce rising costs and create healthier employees. Consumers need to know how these programs can help them take control of their health and how to access available programs.

3. Accessing care. Going to the doctor or the hospital is something many of us dread. Choosing the right doctor, setting up the appointment, filling out the repetitive paper forms, waiting to be examined, and dealing with the barrage of associated paperwork from the doctor and your health plan all make the hassle factor seem overwhelming. Before, during and after the care experience we are often ill-equipped to make good decisions. Before going to the doctor's office, do you have at your fingertips your medical history, prescriptions and health profile information? Do you know which doctors "participate" with your health plan, whether your visit will be covered and, if so, how much it will cost you? While there, do you clearly understand your treatment options and the potential trade-offs between cost, quality and effectiveness of the choices you have to make? When you leave, do you know how much you will be charged for the services you just received, and do you have an agreed-upon follow-up plan with your doctor beyond "take two aspirins and call me in the morning?" We need a common, shared "source of truth" between consumers and providers before, during and after care is delivered to provide more "transparent" information and close the knowledge gap between patients and their doctors, enabling better-informed decision-making.

4. Seeking assistance with questions. As healthcare consumers, we often have questions about our benefits and care. Today, we typically contact our health plan only for administrative issues such as ordering a replacement ID card, changing demographic data such as address or phone number, or inquiring about the virtually unintelligible paperwork we received in the mail related to our last doctor visit. As our responsibilities increase, requiring us to make decisions about coverage options, how to pay for healthcare and where to seek care, we have new needs for support and we have new questions. To whom will we turn for assistance? While many people indicate they don't have complete trust in health plans, health plans are the best "source of truth" for many of these questions. How equipped is your doctor to answer these types of questions? While it may not seem obvious today, many health plans are going through a transformation to be able to better support consumers through these increasingly complex decisions. For many consumers a health coach or healthcare financial planning specialist is just a phone call away. Health plans are beginning an evolution that I believe will be very similar to the evolution that the financial services/banking industry underwent in the 1990s. If you can remember a time when banks were open only from 9 a.m. to 5 p.m. Monday through Friday, ask yourself if you could have foreseen a time when these same banks, which did little more than process checks, make loans and mail us monthly statements, would evolve into full-service financial planning and services companies, with round-the-clock, technology-enabled customer service and support?

Healthcare through the eyes of providers—
doctors, hospitals and pharmacies

From the time we are young, many of us dream of becoming doctors, nurses, or other medical professionals. Health professionals must invest a tremendous amount of time and money in order to receive the education and training necessary for their chosen specialty. As a result, they have a very real need to earn a livelihood that justifies the time and money they have invested in their education and training. The American Medical Association estimates that medical students owe, on average, $140,000 upon graduation.[10] This enormous debt is one reason some medical students look to the greener pastures of specialty care, where they are often better compensated.[11]

While they have been trained in the science of medicine, providers are often unprepared for the incredibly complex "business" side of healthcare. Ultimately the money collected for delivering care needs to be sufficient to fund operations and provide an appropriate level of profit. Revenues must be sufficient to pay the medical professionals and office staff, cover the rent and the cost of malpractice insurance, buy supplies and equipment, and maintain the technology they need to deliver care and manage the business. This business reality may directly impact the patient's experience in the care setting. For example, if you have ever felt that your time with your physician was rushed, your doctor may have been attempting to balance her desire to spend time with you against real economic pressures to maximize patient volume. As the saying goes, "time is money." It is virtually impossible for most providers, particularly those in smaller settings, to separate the science of practicing medicine from the business of being reimbursed for care.

Like consumers, providers also have a lifecycle that accounts for their interactions with the health plan as well as with the patients they treat. The four primary steps in the lifecycle are as follows: *contracting with health plans, scheduling/preparing for patient visits, providing care, and getting paid.*

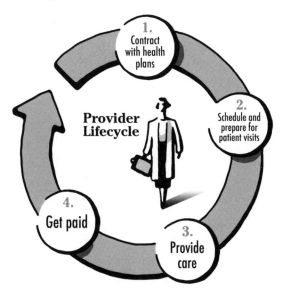

1. Contracting with the health plan. When providers deliver goods or services, they have two sources of income: you (the patient) and, for those patients who have health coverage, the health plan. How much they are paid by a health plan for a specific procedure is determined by a negotiated "fee schedule" contract between the provider and the plan. This price negotiation process is an incredibly important part of the provider lifecycle as it sets the financial criteria that will drive the provider's economic success. In most parts of the country, one provider may have contracts with a dozen or more health plans, as well as with Medicare and Medicaid. That is a dozen or more negotiations and a dozen or more different agreements for payment for each different procedure, introducing administrative complexity that will have ripple effects throughout your experience as a patient.

2. Scheduling and preparing for the patient visit. Before each patient visit, providers must validate the patient's eligibility for healthcare coverage and gather any relevant medical history. Today, much of this process is manual. We are all too familiar with providing our medical background by "filling out the forms on the clipboard." It is important to remember that in many cases, providers very much work in a cottage industry with little technological support around them to help them share information.

When it comes to your patient medical history, providers face a blind spot. They are dependent upon information you as a patient volunteer, as well as whatever information exists within your "chart"—the history of your care within that medical practice. Doctors have very little ability to access data outside of that care setting, including information from other physicians you have seen, lab and imaging tests you have had, or medications you are taking. Providers express a tremendous desire for automation in this and other areas. Increasingly, health plans are enabling real-time access to information about patient eligibility, medical history, treatment plans and patient financial responsibility at the point of service. There are substantial national efforts under way for both physician offices and hospitals to capture and distribute clinical information in electronic health records that can "talk" to one another, but it will be many years before that goal is fully realized. Another movement afoot is an effort to create a personal health record for every patient in the United States. Such a health record would contain historical information about all of the treatments a patient has received from all providers. In the immediate term, the most practical and broad-based "patient record" is a payer-enabled personal health record, as the data required to populate such a record and the ability to share it with the patient and provider already exist within the payers' information systems.

3. Providing care. During the visit, doctors must balance the pressure to see more patients with the desire to spend the time to diagnose and treat each one. With the proliferation of the Internet, you and I can find dozens of sites to help us diagnose and form an opinion about which care option is best for us. Imagine, as a doctor, having to deal with dozens of self-diagnosed patients each day. While it is commendable that patients want to come prepared to the doctor's visit, the danger is that patients sometimes latch onto treatment options that are not covered under their particular health benefits package or that might be ineffective or dangerous given the patient's individual health status, age or medical condition. Providers also face more pressure from private and government payers to follow best practices throughout the care process. In addition, primary care doctors face a proliferation of substitute services such as retail-sited clinics staffed by nurses or nurse practitioners, similarly staffed on-site corporate clinics and hybrid health plan models where certain portions of the patient population become medically managed by the health plan's own physicians once certain health conditions arise.

In addition, doctors are being asked to take a broader role in the health of their patients, not only seeing them in the care setting, but also extending their involvement to include interactions in support of prevention and wellness, as well as coordinating patient care across multiple care settings. Even the definition of a "visit" is changing as doctors begin to consult with their patients by phone or the Web. Whatever the circumstances, providers and their patients need information that is relevant and personalized for specific sets of circumstances.

4. Getting paid. As we touched on in the beginning of this section and in greater detail in Chapter Four, today's healthcare reimbursement mechanisms pay primarily based upon the number of "procedures" done by a physician in a particular setting. The amount of reimbursement is determined by the number of procedures "produced" (or performed) and the "price" that is collected for each procedure produced. Sounds simple enough, right? However, few people understand how complex this system actually is: The amount received for a particular procedure, and who will pay it, varies from patient to patient based upon the health insurance plan (and the contracting process we discussed in step one of the provider lifecycle). Imagine running a business where the price of your product or service varies for each customer. Further imagine that neither you nor your customer knows the price or who is going to pay for the good or service until days, weeks or months after it is provided or consumed. Such is the case in healthcare.

As patients share more and more of the cost of physician payment, doctors face new business problems. Without accurate information about who pays what share of a procedure or office visit, the practice may not realize that the patient is responsible for the majority of the bill. If the provider does not collect the patient's money when care is provided at the "point of service," the amount he actually does collect is likely to be less. In addition, the cost of collecting the money owed is likely to go up, especially if collection agencies need to be hired. The end result is that providers may face new cash flow problems, negatively impacting their business success.

The changing role of employers in health benefits

The majority of Americans who have healthcare insurance obtain their coverage through their employers, who historically have paid the lion's share of the cost of coverage as part of their employees' total compensation package. Employers consider competitive health benefits critical to attracting and retaining a talented workforce and to keeping employees effective and productive in the workplace.

Over the past 10 years, healthcare costs have skyrocketed. For employers, offering healthcare coverage has become a significant challenge in an increasingly competitive global market. The cost of providing healthcare coverage to employees is ultimately reflected in the price of the employers' goods and services. Employers face tough decisions. Most are proportionately sharing these cost increases with their employees. Many have been forced to reduce the level of coverage they offer, and a growing number cannot afford to offer benefits at all.

While healthcare premiums continue to grow at a disproportionate rate, there has been little demonstrable improvement in the results the healthcare system delivers. Hence, employers are questioning the value they are receiving and have begun to demand more value from the entire healthcare system. The existing health benefits model is largely focused on the administrative processes related to enrolling employees in coverage and processing claims when they use the system. It does relatively little to help promote health or manage existing illness, which would better address the employer's goal of keeping employees healthy and productive.

Walking in the shoes of an employer throughout the healthcare lifecycle is one way to better understand how the affordability crisis is fundamentally changing the employer's role. The employer's lifecycle includes four key steps: *determining and selecting benefits, enrolling employees, managing employee health and managing/tracking benefits.*

1. Determining and selecting benefits. Health benefits management is a big job. While many large companies have dedicated benefits managers, many small businesses outsource benefit management or must take a "do-it-yourself" approach. Each year companies must take a hard look at their health benefits and make decisions about whether to continue with their current health plan relationships and benefit offerings or to make changes.

Most small and mid-sized employers work with benefits consultants or brokers. Larger employers may work directly with benefits consultants or the payers' sales staffs. They work together to examine the demographics of the workforce and the financial objectives of the employers. Based upon the size and composition of the workforce, health plans submit proposals they believe meet the benefit level and price point the employer wants or needs. The employer then must decide whether to stay with the existing plan choices or pick new ones. In general, employers may offer their employees several benefit/price combinations from the chosen health plan, but they rarely offer competing choices from two or more different plans. Once they have made a choice, they work with the broker or payer to "set up" the benefits within the health plan's information systems, in preparation for the employee enrollment process.

2. Enrolling employees. Once the set-up process is completed, it is time to enroll employees in their choice of benefits through a process called open enrollment. During this process, employees are educated about the benefit options and any prerequisites, like health risk assessments or health screenings. The administrative tasks and paperwork involved in educating employees on their benefit options and enrolling them and their family members in health benefit plans can be cumbersome for any employer. As a result, many employers have adopted technology solutions that facilitate the employee benefit selection and enrollment processes. Once employees have selected their desired level of benefits, employers work with the broker or health plan to enter this information into the payers' information systems, which ultimately produce ID cards that will be delivered to the employees as evidence of health coverage when they go to a doctor or hospital.

3. Managing employee health. Having healthy and effective employees is the purpose of providing employee health benefit coverage. After all, healthy employees are more productive and use fewer sick days. Because employee absenteeism in the American workplace costs companies billions of dollars in lost revenue and productivity, employers are looking for benefit plan designs that promote health and wellness, rather than plans that simply treat illness. In collaboration with their health plans, employers are increasingly providing the information and incentives that employees need to manage their own health more actively. Employers are changing how they view healthcare and are taking action to promote a culture of health. Within the workplace, some employers offer fitness centers, health fairs, and cafeterias filled with healthy food options, in an effort to promote health and wellness. Others may pay cash rewards to employees who achieve weight loss goals. And some even provide a premium "holiday," waiving some portion of the premium for employees who complete health risk assessments.

4. Managing/tracking benefits. Throughout the course of the year, employers must manage and track the benefits of the company's employees. Any time an employee's "status" changes, whether it's due to the birth of a child, a move to another location, or even termination of employment, there are implications not only for the employee's eligibility status but also for the company's premium payments to the health plan. This monthly process of reconciliation of eligibility and payments requires ongoing time and effort. Moreover, the employer's health benefit administrators often act as the first level of customer service, triaging calls from employees who have healthcare questions. Employers need tools to help streamline and manage these processes.

In addition to the monthly reconciliation process, employers track the effectiveness and value of their employee benefit coverage over the course of the year. They ask questions such as: Is our healthcare utilization going up or down? Are employees healthier overall? Are they satisfied with the health plan's service? When it comes time for the annual contract renewal process, the answers to these questions will drive whether or not the employer stays with the same health plan or shops for a new one. Ultimately employers need benefit designs that help slow the rate of premium growth, or even reduce the cost of providing healthcare coverage. Sadly, if real progress is not made regarding the value delivered by the healthcare system, employers will be compelled to minimize their role, perhaps even washing their hands of involvement in selecting and funding health benefits. If employers reduce involvement, more consumers will find themselves in the middle of the healthcare jungle with one less advocate to help them navigate.

Brokers enable effective distribution of health benefits
Earlier in this chapter, we examined the importance of healthcare purchasing decisions in the context of both the employer and the consumer. Brokers play an important role in helping consumers and employers decide which health plan company and what types of benefits will best meet their needs. With over one million licensed health and life insurance brokers in the nation,[12] they are a big part of the healthcare supply chain.

Brokers bring health benefit buyers and sellers together. They earn their customers (individuals and employers) by offering competitive health benefit products from health plans and by providing services that assist with the selection, enrollment and ongoing support of the chosen health benefit products.

Brokers are paid a commission by the health plans in exchange for the "book of business" they deliver and for the services they provide to support their clients. Essentially, they are an extension of both the sales force and customer service units of the health plan. Ultimately, brokers want competitive products to sell from health plans that deliver high levels of quality and service. And they want their customers to renew their contracts with their existing health plans, instead of repeating the costly selection/replacement process on a frequent basis.

The lifecycle of brokers parallels that of employers and includes four key responsibilities: *evaluating and selecting health plans, educating and enrolling employees, advocating employee health, and managing service and costs.*

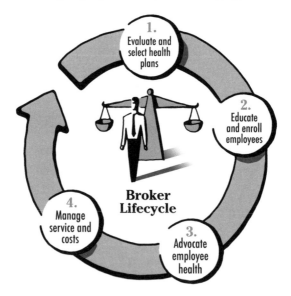

1. Evaluating and selecting the health plan. Brokers want products that meet their clients' needs, which include health and wellness coverage at a reasonable cost. While cost is a big factor in whether brokers will recommend a particular health plan to their employer clients, brokers usually do not recommend health plans based on cost alone. Rather, brokers look for heath plans that can differentiate themselves in several ways. Specifically, they look for benefit plan designs that drive down medical costs, information technology tools that reduce paperwork, and service offerings (such as health coaches) that will enhance customer satisfaction. Evaluating and selecting the right health plan for an employer requires that brokers not only understand the plan's benefit offering, but also that they understand the tools and services the health plan provides to help control costs and improve customer satisfaction. Brokers ultimately drive more business to those health plans that do a good job of educating and collaborating with them and with consumers, as well as providing the tools that make the selling process easier—for example, financial modeling tools and personalized education materials. This is true for new sales as well as renewals of existing contracts, which require less effort by brokers than starting from scratch.

2. Educating and enrolling employees. In order to increase their chances of renewing existing contracts, brokers need to provide excellent service to their customers. To this end, they need tools that streamline enrollment and help consumers choose providers based on data about quality. On-line enrollment capabilities reduce the administrative burden for employers (by eliminating paper applications) and often serve as a mechanism for educating employees on their cost trade-offs. Brokers also examine the availability of disease management and health and wellness programs that can be efficiently introduced in conjunction with the enrollment process.

3. Advocating employee health. In addition to helping employers navigate their choices and select and enroll in a health plan, brokers increasingly seek to play the role of "employee advocate," offering assistance in promoting a culture of health. For example, brokers have become more involved in monitoring trends within the employer's employee population. Are people getting healthier? Is medical utilization up or down? Are employees participating in available health and wellness programs? If not, why not? The answers to questions such as these play a key role in helping employers decide how to modify next year's benefit design and health plan.

4. Managing service and costs. The work of a broker, like that of an employer, does not stop once employees are enrolled in the health plan. Brokers spend their time after enrollment monitoring the status of their accounts, including costs, utilization levels and customer satisfaction. To that end, brokers depend on reporting tools for each of their accounts. They also provide ongoing service to their employer accounts, including solving billing, eligibility and claims problems. They add value by doing the legwork for their clients and making sure those clients get the most from their coverage after they've bought it. When a client has chosen a self-funded plan, brokers periodically review whether the actual amount being spent on healthcare is consistent with original assumptions for that employee population.

Health plans as supply chain facilitators

Although sometimes publicly maligned, health plans are managed and operated by human beings who are as intent on providing high-quality healthcare to the members of their plans as are the doctors, nurses and other providers who deliver the care. The success of their business is measured in terms of how many members belong to their plan, which is considered a function of the benefit options, price, and health management and administrative service levels the health plan offers.

As organizers of the healthcare supply chain, health plans are at the center of the interactions among the healthcare constituents and facilitate the administrative processes that support their collective set of lifecycles. Within the health plan's own lifecycle, there are eight key business processes that support and facilitate the healthcare supply chain:

- *Product Development* is the process of designing the health benefit "products"—such as a high-deductible plan with a health savings account, or a Medicare Advantage plan—to be sold to employers, brokers and consumers. This process is a precursor to step one in the employer, broker and consumer lifecycles related to evaluating and selecting plans.

- *Risk Management* includes actuarial, underwriting and other analytical functions that determine health benefit pricing during product design and the selling process. This process is a precursor to step one in the employer, broker and consumer lifecycles related to evaluating and selecting plans.

- *Revenue Management* includes the processes to support health benefit sales, employer group set-up, member enrollment and the ongoing collection of premiums. This process directly supports step one in the employer, broker and consumer lifecycles related to evaluating and selecting plans.

- *Customer Service* includes the processes for providing ongoing support and assistance to each of the constituents across their respective lifecycles. This process is highlighted for consumers in the *Seeking Assistance with Questions* lifecycle step but pertains to servicing each of the constituents.

- *Reimbursement Management* includes the accurate and timely payment of claims to physicians, hospitals and pharmacies as well as determining what portion of financial responsibility resides with the consumer. It begins with verification of eligibility and ends when the full contractual amount is paid. This is reflected in the *Schedule and Prepare for Visits* and the *Get Paid* lifecycle steps for providers as well as the *Access Care* lifecycle step for consumers.

- *Care Management* includes the processes involved in managing consumer health and assisting in seeking effective and appropriate care. The health plan care management process is reflected in the consumer's *Staying Healthy* and *Accessing Care* lifecycle steps and the provider's *Scheduling/Preparing for Patient Visit* and *Providing Care* lifecycle steps.

- *Network Management* is the set of processes involved in contracting with providers to create the provider network and establish pre-arranged pricing discounts on behalf of members and employers. This process is highlighted in the provider's *Contracting with Health Plans* lifecycle step.

- *Finance and Administration* are internal financial processes required to run an organized system of benefits and care, including infrastructure comprising people and sophisticated information technology.

These process descriptions provide a quick snapshot of what is required by health plans to organize and manage the healthcare supply chain and to provide products, services and support for each of the constituents across their lifecycles. As we seek a more systematic design for healthcare and the interactions among constituents, these processes will have to be modified to facilitate change.

Over the past decade, health plans have focused largely on driving down administrative costs within their operations. Widespread investment in technology to efficiently enroll members and pay claims has been a top priority and has returned impressive results. However, as the cost of care delivery continues to increase, many health plans are playing a more active role in helping to manage the cost and quality of care delivery. It is clear from examining the complex needs of healthcare constituents that health plans can indeed add significant incremental value by designing a system to facilitate information flow, improve interactions among all constituents, and develop incentives that are aligned to reward behaviors that lead to better health. Managed care principles employed in the late 1980s and early 1990s proved costs can be effectively controlled but did so with restrictions on convenience and choice that many found unpalatable. And yet, providers, employers and government policymakers acknowledge that the managed care concepts of population management (such as segmentation) and organized networks of care providers make sense today. The challenge currently being examined by health plans is how to effectively manage both cost and quality of care, but this time in a manner that involves partnership and vested buy-in on the part of all constituents. It is a systematic challenge that must and will be solved.

As you will learn in the next chapter, a wealth of key information that can add value to the healthcare experience exists in the physical and electronic files and databases of consumers, providers, payers, employers and brokers. The challenge is that much of it is stored in isolated silos, with no easy way to share information among these constituents.

• • • • • • • • • • • • •

CHAPTER SIX

Sub-Optimized Silos: Information Isolation

Knowledge is like money: to be of value, it must circulate, and in circulation it can increase in quantity, and hopefully in value.

– Louis L'Amour

Do you have a club card for your favorite grocery store chain? If you do, you know that no matter which location you visit, the system knows you—giving you your frequent-shopper discount and crediting points to your account. In addition, at check-out time you likely receive coupons for items you have bought in the past or for competitive products in the same category, based on promotional agreements the store has in place with various manufacturers and distributors. These stores do a good job of systematically collecting data about you, such as your past purchases, spending levels and method of payment. They also know your address, ZIP code and phone number. They combine this data into useful information that allows them to customize offers intended to create value for you and build loyalty.

Believe it or not, the U.S. healthcare system collects far more data about you than does your grocery store. Yet most grocery chains do a better job than our healthcare system of leveraging and utilizing information to conveniently serve consumers. What is behind this difference? In our healthcare system, much of the collected data is locked up in *information silos* and neither shared with the people who need it nor combined with other information to unlock the data's full power. Just as each farm stores its own grain in an individual silo, countless pieces of data are collected within the healthcare system about you and your family, used quickly for one or two transactions (such as to process your claim or issue your ID card) and then stored in a computer or file cabinet where they might never be used again.

Redundancy—the biggest irritant in healthcare

Perhaps the most obvious example of how information silos affect you is the insidious paper form (mentioned earlier in this book) that you are asked to complete every time you see a different doctor or go to an emergency room. In this age of technology, when a retailer can take information you supply and use it to recognize you every time you enter any branch of the store, it is hard to believe the healthcare system is not set up to share basic information contained on an intake form, particularly if you have health insurance. Imagine what it would be like if you could complete a detailed, carefully developed form once, preferably on-line, and this information could be made available throughout the healthcare system, as appropriate. Not only is it annoying and inefficient to have to complete the same form over and over, but the fact that important information is not being shared and used to its full potential is both expensive and dangerous.

At the writing of this book, Congress has created legislation to fund and promote electronic health records for digitally storing and ultimately sharing information among different healthcare providers. (See Chapter Nine for more detail.) But the provider-only approach being contemplated—while helpful to the important issue of patient safety—will take more than a decade to achieve a meaningful impact on solving healthcare cost and total quality issues because it is not systematic and fails to fully connect the supply chain we learned about in Chapter Four. As we all know, it takes time to integrate people, processes and technology. (Remember my earlier comment on paving cow paths: Simply digitizing a fragmented system will not fix it.) But despite the long lead time for implementation, let me be clear that electronic health records are a move in the right direction. Obviously, when your grocery store knows more about you simply from your phone number than does the healthcare system, in spite of your many interactions with it, something needs to change.

Information silo basics

Without overcomplicating the issue, data assembled to accomplish something useful is information. For example, when a store's information technology analyzes your shopping history (the data) against available coupon promotions, it results in useful information about what type of coupon to print on the back of your grocery receipt. Information scientists also talk about knowledge (applying what is learned from information) and wisdom (knowing when seemingly good information or conventional knowledge is faulty or out of context). For purposes of this chapter, we will use the term "information" to represent the broader spectrum.

There are over 200 million people in the United States who receive health coverage in organized systems of benefits and care. But what is known about each person? Quite a lot is known; however, this information exists in information silos that fall into three main areas: core benefit administration, care management, and constituent information.

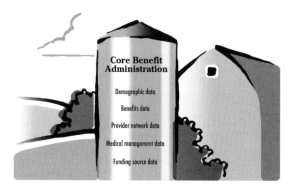

The core benefit administration silo: demographics, benefits,
provider networks medical management and funding sources
Demographic data includes your name, age, address, other family members
covered by your health plan, etc. Benefits data includes your employer, your
covered health benefits, your insurance premium amount, your claims history
including your diagnoses, procedures you have received to date, where and
when and by whom the procedures were performed, your prescription drug
history, as well as a host of other data. Provider network data keeps track of
which doctors, hospitals, diagnostic centers and pharmacies are "in network"
along with the pre-contracted pricing for each type of service or therapy.
Medical management data supplements benefits data and keeps track of what
benefits you are able to access on your own and what benefits require additional
permissions (or referrals). Funding source data includes the types of funding mechanisms each consumer can use to help pay for healthcare, whether
through pre-tax dollars such as health savings accounts (HSAs) and flexible
spending accounts (FSAs), or healthcare subsidies available from government
agencies such as the State Children's Health Insurance Program (SCHIP).
Though these arrangements vary, they are all tools to help consumers pay for
medical expenses.

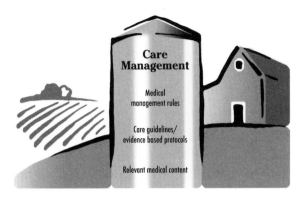

The care management silo: rules, protocols and information to support high-quality care

The second silo of information is called care management. Simply put, this category consists of data intended to ensure that you receive good care for a given cost. It includes the rules and guidelines established by your health plan (called *medical management rules*); the documented "best practices" or most effective courses of treatment for various medical conditions (called care guidelines or *evidence-based protocols*); and relevant medical content—additional medical information needed to assist you and your doctor in making good decisions about managing your care. The care management information silo is both scientifically and politically explosive. The body of evidence-based science grows at an astonishing rate, and as you can imagine, is subject to change every time a new drug is approved, a new device or surgical technique is developed, and increasingly, as genomics teaches us how to evaluate the efficacy of one treatment versus another at the individual genetic level. Discussion about when to use scientific evidence-based protocols in the practice of medicine by physicians with many years of training and experience has created tension and continues to cause payers and providers to challenge one another as to who should determine what is appropriate.

The medical management rules issued by health plans can determine what care a provider is able to give you (and be reimbursed). For example, your primary care doctor is authorized by the health plan to evaluate and monitor your overall health and make referrals to specialists when appropriate but he or she is not authorized to perform a hip replacement or prescribe an experimental drug. Other medical management rules address your cost of receiving care at various care settings. For example, you generally pay a moderate co-payment if you have your sore throat treated at your doctor's office; however, if you go to the emergency room for a bad cold or sore throat, you will usually be charged much more out-of-pocket because emergency rooms are one of the most expensive places to receive care. The mailing you received when you enrolled in your health plan probably warned you that the emergency room is for emergencies only. A lack of knowledge about the rules for when and where to seek various types of care, combined with few incentives to follow the rules is one reason for today's soaring healthcare costs. (We'll talk more about incentives in the next two chapters.)

Evidence-based protocols are another important part of the care management silo. These protocols have been developed based on a growing body of medical research on the effectiveness of various treatments for specific illnesses, conditions and injuries. Dr. Jack Wennberg and his colleagues, in the Dartmouth Atlas of Health Care, pioneered the evaluation of medical practice variations and comparative effectiveness and demonstrated that more care is not necessarily the best care. Today, many doctors receive updates on this "best practice" information but it is not widely distributed in a format doctors can access in a timely manner or use to communicate efficiently with their patients.

Contrast these doctors to the Lexus technicians, who can access historical records as well as the recommended treatment protocols (including parts and pricing) to repair or perform preventive maintenance on an automobile. Doctors and patients need clear information about what the best approach is, given the patient's diagnosis, medical history, life stage, and other information. In cases where there are several possible approaches or procedures, they need to be able to compare the potential risks and rewards of each course of treatment. The lack of clear and understandable information has resulted in a high degree of variation in medical practice, outcomes and cost. Moreover, if patients do not understand why one particular medical approach has been shown to be more effective for their particular situation than another procedure they found on the Internet, they might think that their doctor or health plan is denying them that care simply to save money rather than because the procedure in question has not been shown to be as effective in patients with similar medical histories and of comparable age and health status.

In addition to medical management rules and evidence-based protocols, there is other medical information that completes the care management information silo. One example is printed or Web-based healthcare content that can educate and assist you in making informed decisions. Perhaps you are also beginning to recognize from a systematic standpoint that "administrative" data about what benefits you've received is also a rich source of care management data, and that all care management information is most relevant if it is put into the context of your specific benefit plan and your particular provider network—rather than presented in general terms.

This would be a good time to mention that vast amounts of data exist in care settings themselves, such as physician offices and hospitals. These entities have a broad variety of clinical information systems to aid in the practice of medicine and the delivery of care to patients. In addition, physicians, nurses and other caregivers have extensive amounts of training, knowledge and experience that they apply during the process of delivering care. Because this data exists "in their heads" and is not documented in an organized way, it perpetuates the locking of information within silos. As we will see later, knowledge that is not shared can promote misaligned incentives in the healthcare system.

The constituent information silo: data about
uniqueness, preferences and attitudes

The third information silo is called constituent information. As its name suggests, it includes unique, descriptive information that is captured or inferred about a person within the healthcare system—whether he is a consumer, provider, employer, or broker. It is important to understand that in a system with millions of consumers, hundreds of thousands of providers, and countless other stakeholders, constituent information is key to designing a systematic process that optimizes benefits and care.

In the case of consumers, much of this information is contained inside their heads and known to few others. Some examples include information about whether a person lives alone or has people around to help with medical care or transportation; whether she prefers to communicate by cell phone, on-line or by mail; and her educational level and income. Doctors have patients with very different sets of needs and constraints. This constituent information can help doctors develop treatment plans that will work best for a particular patient's situation. For example, a 39-year-old single working mother of four who is living just above the income threshold for being Medicaid-eligible probably needs care for herself and her family at the lowest possible cost. To avoid missing work, she might need to get her care after hours. She also may prefer to go to a clinic or hospital near her house if she needs to have lab tests done. And she may not have reliable access to computer or cell phone technology as a means of getting health information. In contrast, a 28-year-old married lawyer with no children probably has fewer constraints as to when and where she can go for care, and cost may not be as much of a factor in determining her treatment. She probably can rely on her spouse in the event she cannot transport herself to a physical therapy appointment or for a lab test. In addition, she very likely relies heavily on her cell phone and computer as a means of receiving information and would benefit from tools like on-line scheduling. A doctor who sees both of these patients and who has accurate constituent information about each person has the opportunity to tailor their respective care plans in ways that not only are most convenient but also have the best chance of being followed.

Although consumers may be the most obvious suppliers of constituent information, other constituents can also supply valuable information about themselves. For example, doctors might have useful information about their education, areas of specialization, which languages they speak, whether they are accepting new patients, and their office hours. Brokers can supply information about the languages they speak, the list of health plans for which they are able to provide quotes, and whether they provide any kind of health or wellness services to assist their clients. Employers have information about whether they provide injury prevention and wellness programs and whether they can answer benefits questions or must rely upon brokers for this service.

Healthcare evolution versus systematic design

Clearly, a wealth of information in the three information silos is captured and stored every day somewhere in the healthcare system, but it is fragmented and separated instead of being accessible to all who need it. This fragmentation is no surprise given the history of the U.S. healthcare system. As we have seen in previous chapters, the healthcare system has evolved over time from a model where actuaries tried to predict annual costs and then crossed their fingers in the hope that actual claims submitted by doctors, hospitals and pharmacies would not exceed the premium amounts charged to consumers, toward an organized supply chain model that has attempted to create a higher degree of predictability of cost and quality.

While we have come a long way since the early days of insurance, we still have a long way to go. Healthcare in total has only sporadically been engineered as a system in the same way as a first-rate auto manufacturer or a big-box retail store. Consequently, information collection and storage has not been systematically designed to support a common set of rules that can be shared among brokers and employers. Many managed care organizations have attempted to do just this since the mid-1980s. As we've discussed, however, coordinated change across people, processes and technologies is challenging. And rather than trying to find managed care successes that worked in many areas of the country, it became politically expedient to malign the whole attempt at systematic change. In other words, the baby was thrown out with the bath water. Because all the constituents have not agreed on a basic common approach, each constituent has structured its own information collection based on the specific tasks it must accomplish—much like the assembly lines that were used by early American automobile manufacturers. For payers, the goals are to bill the right premium amount to each employer for its employees, to pay out the approved amount for each claim, to issue ID cards, and to respond to questions from consumers. Doctors have the goal of being reimbursed by following health plan rules while also providing the best care possible. Hospitals and pharmacies have structured their information collection and storage around still other specific goals, as have all of the other healthcare constituents. But there is far too little information crossover among these functional areas. Employers and brokers need information about the effectiveness of health and wellness programs and about the status of their employees and clients.

Adding to the fragmented evolution is the fact that constituents are looking at healthcare from different perspectives, as described in Chapter Five. Doctors study medicine empirically and are generally not systems designers. Employers want productive, healthy employees at reasonable costs. Brokers try to bring order to chaos and match consumers and employers to the best plan that fits their budget. And consumers seek access to care when they need it and coverage to help pay for it. Only payers are weaving together a supply chain of staggering complexity while trying to please all constituents. But as I mentioned earlier, they generally get roundly criticized for imposing organizing principles and systematic constraints.

Disconnect between core benefit administration and care management

The information silo concept becomes even more obvious once you walk through the door of the waiting room and enter the world of care. In order to provide the best care possible, each doctor, physical therapist or other healthcare professional ideally needs to know what care has already been administered to the consumer by others. However, if each provider collects and stores consumer health information in an isolated paper medical record (or even an electronic one), the other providers cannot access important information on medications being taken, prior surgeries, allergic reactions and chronic health conditions, all of which would help the provider deliver the best care possible.

For example, if you forget to tell your neurologist that your primary care doctor prescribed sleeping pills for you last week, your neurologist will be missing a critical piece of information. He may decide on one course of treatment based on the assumption that you are not on any other medications but he might have made a different decision if he had known you were already taking the sleeping pills. It may surprise you to know that your health plan has a prescription benefits management function that keeps a record of every prescription you have filled as well as which doctors wrote the prescriptions. The health plan collects this data in order to accomplish its administrative goal of issuing proper payment for covered services. The problem is that the information is locked up in that administrative silo and the health plan has never been instructed to share this type of information with other parts of the system that would find it useful. But as I mentioned earlier, simply making the data available in an electronic record does not solve the problem. The doctor would deliberately have to change his or her workflow in order for this information to improve the quality of healthcare at a given cost.

Another example of providers of care not having access to important information in the core benefit administration silo came up when I needed a referral to see a specialist. My doctor considered my specific situation and gave me the names of two highly regarded otolaryngologists (i.e., ear, nose and throat specialists). Knowing the healthcare jungle as I do, I naturally asked the nurse calling with the referral to ask whether these specialists were on my health plan's panel of physicians. It turned out that only one of them was in my health plan's provider network, and that is who I went to. Had I not known to ask, my referral may well have been to a physician who is not part of my pre-contracted provider network and I would have had to pay much more for the same service.

Earlier in this book, we saw other examples of information not being systematically shared, such as when a patient moves to another state and forgets to have his former doctor send his medical records to a new doctor. We have also learned about the frightening results of an emergency room not having access to a patient's medical record to check for a drug allergy or interaction between a drug already being taken and one the ER administers. There are countless other examples of serious medical errors and wasted money that occur because information is not shared among the parts of the healthcare system.

A health information aggregator is key

Given how important the sharing of information is in receiving good care, it is incomprehensible that most consumers lack a way to keep track of their health histories as they travel through the healthcare system over a lifetime. After all, we have statements for our bank accounts and investments, which provide detailed information on all account activity within a given period of time. Even college students have a record of all of the classes they have taken, their grades, and any withdrawals or incompletes. As a nation, we do an excellent job of keeping track of important information in so many areas of our lives. However, we fall inexcusably short in the one area where we are guaranteed to amass information from birth until death and where tracking and sharing information could make the difference between life and death.

As I mentioned previously, one important tool that is just beginning to take root is the *personal health record*, an updatable record of all the care a patient receives. It can be accessed by the patient and, with permission, by providers and other caregivers whenever and wherever the patient receives care or medical services. The consumer can see his complete health history, relevant financial data such as balances in funding source accounts and how much money was used last year, and providers can see what prescriptions and procedures have been provided by other medical professionals. There is much discussion in healthcare policy circles about both personal health records and their close digital cousins, electronic health records, but so far they have been implemented only on a limited basis. The distinctions between these tools are described further in Chapter Nine.

Silos obscure pricing information

As the affordability crisis worsens and employers look for new ways to cut costs while continuing to provide health benefits to their employees, more consumers will find themselves having to manage not only their health but also the cost of their healthcare. Those of us who have health plans where we pay a small co-payment and leave the rest of the cost of our care to our health plans will find that we are a dwindling species. As more employers offer health plans with lower premiums paired with greater consumer responsibility for out-of-pocket costs, consumers will need information about the actual cost of procedures, hospitalization, office visits and prescription drugs. Similarly, providers will need better information about how much the consumer should pay them while in the office and how much the health plan will cover.

Consumer-directed health plans are the most obvious example of where more information is needed. In these types of plans the consumer does not pay a co-payment at the beginning of a new year. Instead, he is responsible for the full cost of his care up to a certain dollar amount—his deductible. As the system is set up now, the patient with a sore throat goes to the doctor and incurs a charge of, say, $100. The doctor's office can see that the patient has Health Plan X but has no idea how much of the $100 office visit will be covered by the health plan. All of the key information about the patient's benefit plan and whether he has reached his deductible (in which case the health plan coverage would kick in) exists in the health plan's core benefit administration silo. In many cases such as this, the patient gets care and goes home not having paid a cent. The doctor is then stuck with a job she never trained for and to which she certainly never aspired—that of payment collector. Also, because patient liability information is not shared with the doctor's office, more paperwork is generated, consumer debt increases, and the doctor accumulates large amounts of accounts receivable, making it difficult to keep up with ongoing operating expenses.

Access to "real" cost information is extremely important to most consumers who are responsible for paying for the total cost of their care before reaching their deductible and then for paying a portion thereafter. Currently, their situation is analogous to going to a restaurant having only a fixed budget in your wallet and ordering from the menu without knowing how much each item costs. Again, the information about price exists in the healthcare system but is not available to the consumer who has to decide how to spend a finite amount of money. It is hard to think of any other industry where this model would be acceptable, except for meal plans in college cafeterias. Can you imagine going to Nordstrom's, selecting a pair of shoes without seeing the price, paying the sales clerk $15 and then asking the store to let you know the full price when they bill you for the balance at the end of the month? Even if you have a health plan that uses co-payments and you know the balance of the full cost of care will be covered, it is easy to see that information silos regarding cost contribute to the inefficiency of the healthcare system. The good news is that because most of the information constituents lack is already captured elsewhere in the system, the problem of information silos can most definitely be solved given adequate financial and information system design resources. By knitting together these information silos and enabling information to be available to constituents across the healthcare system, we can create the same transparency that operates in the retail world. Before we can create this convergence, however, we must confront a series of barriers in the way dollars flow through the healthcare system. In Chapter Seven, we'll examine these barriers.

The inefficiency of our healthcare system is caused not only by the problem of fragmented information silos but also by the way financial interactions are set up. In Chapter Seven we'll examine the way financial interactions affect the cost of healthcare and set up a zero-sum game among constituents.

• • • • • • • • • • • • • •

Follow the Dollar

Insanity: doing the same thing over and over
again and expecting different results.
– Attributed to Albert Einstein

Everyone knows that enormous sums of money are spent on healthcare in the United States each year. On that point, there seems to be almost no argument. Likewise, the perceived return we get as a nation at this macro-spending level (i.e., the total value received for the total number of dollars spent across all individuals) is widely viewed as inadequate. This is most often put into the context of healthcare spending as a percentage of gross domestic product (GDP), which at approximately 17 percent in a relatively wealthy nation makes us a big outlier.

It is at this point that the thinking of intelligent leaders throughout our country diverges as industry experts and pundits wrestle with three repetitive themes that take turns on the front pages of numerous publications. First is the perplexing problem that we spend more than anybody else, and yet we still have nearly 50 million people without health insurance. Second is that the relatively higher cost of healthcare coverage for our workers causes U.S. companies to lose their competitive edge in pricing products for an increasingly competitive world market. And third are the statistics I shared with you in Chapter One, whereby the United States posts poorer scores on infant mortality and longevity than do many other developed nations. These are likely all familiar themes to you.

As this is not a book about healthcare economics or healthcare policy, spending a chapter analyzing these points doesn't really help us get to the solution. If we work under the assumption that we want every person in the country to have access to high-quality healthcare at an affordable cost, it's probably best to take a step back from the problem and examine it systematically. And once again, think about drawing on experience from other industries where appropriate. Based on my experience, what I can tell you is that because so few people trying to solve the problem have a comprehensive understanding of the healthcare elephant, you can move from venue to venue of "experts" and quickly realize that there is no common view of the problem—even if the words sound similar. And if you listen carefully, there is always at the least the faint murmur (more often the thunder) of the almighty dollar driving the dialogue and behavior of the group participants—whether by objective or by necessity.

Understanding the basic dollar flow

Until you understand at least the basics of how dollars flow through the healthcare "system" it is difficult to comprehend fully why it works the way it does. So let's follow the dollar through the healthcare jungle and see where it goes. Returning to the supply chain concept from Chapter Four, we begin with the fact that there is a practical need to package the demand for healthcare as well as the suppliers of healthcare into a pre-defined benefits package at a predictable price. Typically, the pricing for this benefit plan comes in the form of an insurance premium, and generally a benefit plan is classified as being either high-deductible or low-deductible. Once the deductible—the amount for which the consumer is responsible before the benefit plan starts paying—is reached, a predictable pattern of dollar distribution begins. This limited number of dollars must somehow be allocated among all of the parts of the system. Because the healthcare industry operates in silos and has never been designed so the parts work systematically in concert, it is not surprising that each part of the system—pharmacies, hospitals, doctors and suppliers—would each vie for a greater proportion of each healthcare dollar. This zero-sum-game behavior is a natural result of competition and constrained resources.

What we must understand about all zero-sum games, however, is that if one player wins additional dollars within a constrained system, other players must collectively lose that same sum. Since as a nation we can't afford to spend more money on a sustainable basis, there are a great many constituents that are going to have to get less—or accomplish more for the same amount. What's important is that this allocation of resources be accomplished systematically, not in a punitive way. I will lay out this methodology in Chapter Eight. For now, let's continue understanding the current dollar flow.

The payer pie: how your insurance works

It is probably most useful to begin with the perspective of the payer, as the bulk of dollars are collected and distributed by the payer. If you are one of the more than 200 million Americans covered by a private insurance plan, your health insurance company collects premiums from your employer, or from you directly, in order to administer your benefits. The illustration below shows how each premium dollar is distributed today.

The Healthcare Dollar
from a Payer Perspective

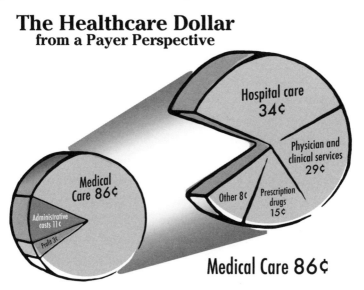

Hospital care
34¢

Physician and
clinical services
29¢

Medical
Care 86¢

Other 8¢

Prescription
drugs
15¢

Administrative
costs 11¢

Profit 3¢

Medical Care 86¢

Approximation based upon data combining Medicare population and com-
mercial data. (Source: Adapted from centers for Medicare and Medicaid
Services [2007] and 2008 Combined Util SEER – Volume II C – General
Edition, Comprehensive Total Summary of Medians, Sherlock Company)

Approximately 11 percent of each premium dollar is used to administer your health benefits. This includes all the typical business processes: designing your benefit plan; putting in place pricing contracts with hospitals, physicians, diagnostic centers, pharmacies and other suppliers; enrolling you in the plan and collecting your premiums; processing and paying submitted claims; delivering customer service to consumers, employers, providers and brokers; providing medical management for the enrolled population; and accounting for all of these activities in order to remain solvent and able to price next year's benefit plans properly. Let me make several observations that may not be obvious to the average consumer. First, in many parts of the country, nearly half of this 11 percent goes to pay for the distribution of the benefit plan product in the form of payment to brokers or producers. Health plans typically have very small sales organizations that deliver information to brokers who issue requests for proposals (RFPs) on behalf of employer groups or who seek health insurance quotes on behalf of individuals. Second, health plans do not charge a mark-up on the claims they pay. In fact, they nearly always pay a discounted price that has been pre-negotiated. And by the way, when you are in your deductible phase or paying out of pocket, you are the beneficiary of these discounted prices. Can you imagine paying the prices that Walmart's suppliers would charge you directly if Walmart had not already negotiated these discounts for you?

So when you think about the next section of the healthcare dollar pie, the approximately 86 percent that is paid directly by the health plan for the provision of medical care, keep in mind that in most cases, the doctors, hospitals, diagnostic centers, pharmacies and suppliers getting paid are not thrilled. They are not thrilled for at least two reasons. The first is that they don't particularly appreciate the fact that "their" patient or customer is actually a member of a health plan and that when it comes to establishing and maintaining the relationship, these providers have to contend with a series of powerful third-party forces (i.e., health plans) that have essentially already carved up the market share in the service areas. The second reason is that in order to receive payment, providers must comply with a series of required data and information submissions or follow certain protocols, in some cases causing them to feel that the health plans are interfering with their ability to practice medicine the way they think is best. Bluntly stated, both concerns have merit. And systematically, the give-and-take friction from perceived obstacles is necessary to create a rational system.

I happen to live near an area where established physicians tend to boldly proclaim that they are going to refuse to accept the discounted fee schedules of leading health plans because they believe their clientele will choose them over their insurance companies. They also believe their patients have the ability on a personal out-of-pocket basis to pay the higher costs that result from the health plan's being left out of the price negotiations. This is a brilliant solution for physicians who exclusively serve the wealthiest two percent of Americans, but it would not work for most doctors. Nor is this a systematically practical solution. If this methodology were applied to the broader population most physicians would spend more time and energy chasing down accounts receivable from patients than they would treating those patients.

The smallest slice of the pie, approximately three percent, is labeled as profit. Without getting into the complex details of pre-tax or after-tax profitability, the point is straightforward. Private health plans expect to earn a profit for being organizers of your healthcare supply chain and delivering what they believe is a solid benefit-plan product at a reasonable price. They believe that they deliver you at least four kinds of value, which entitles them to earn a return on your premium dollar.

First, they offer you pricing value, as you would not be able to negotiate the same discounted rates as an individual that health plans negotiate on your behalf. Second, they offer you an infrastructure so that you do not have to "Yellow Page" your way through the healthcare system to find primary care and specialty physicians, and they facilitate access to physicians, hospitals, diagnostic centers and pharmacies within your health plan network. Third, they offer insurance or risk-mitigation value by providing a backstop against personal financial disaster caused by catastrophic accidents or illness. Fourth, they offer information value, whereby they facilitate your ability to make informed decisions about your benefits and care via printed and on-line information that is relevant to your benefit plan and available provider network.

Based on my experience, these four areas are generally undervalued by virtually everyone except health plan executives, knowledgeable benefits managers, and those who analyze and invest in health plan stocks. But, in my opinion, that is because most other parties don't want to hear or acknowledge the complexity of what it takes to construct an organized system of benefits and care. Most people don't want to hear how Walmart or Federal Express work either; they just want great products at low prices, as well as on-time delivery. Yet there is a fundamental understanding that massive infrastructure is required to run these well-known retail enterprises, while few people think about what it takes to run healthcare organizations such as BlueCross BlueShield affiliates, Aetna, CIGNA, United Health Group and Humana.

"For-profit" and "not-for-profit" both require more dollars in than out
As we follow the dollar through the healthcare system, we must clear up one common misconception. People talk about various parts of the healthcare

system as being "for-profit" or "not-for-profit," with the implication that the former is more apt to contribute to rising healthcare costs than the latter. Listen carefully to casual healthcare conversations. What you may hear is the general assumption that "for-profit" includes most health plans, hospitals that are not church-supported, pharmacies, pharmaceutical companies, medical device manufacturers, and some types of doctors such as surgeons and radiologists. On the other hand, people assume that church-supported hospitals, most doctors, Medicare, Medicaid, and a few health plans make up the "not-for-profit" category. The implication is that the for-profit entities somehow take value away from the system while not-for-profits are neutral at worst.

This assumption is erroneous, because whether a particular entity is for-profit or not-for-profit, it has to bring in more money than it spends or else it will not survive. This is known as an operating margin. In health plans and hospitals alike, the difference in day-to-day operating discipline is virtually undetectable among for-profits and their not-for profit counterparts. Not-for-profits enjoy benefits stemming from federal and state tax codes and they access capital differently than for-profit entities—and particularly in contrast to publicly traded for-profit entities—but the substantial differences really get quite technical in terms of financial reporting and capital-raising. Both types of entities are subject to regulatory oversight that, among other things, requires the establishment of reserves so that financial health can be easily measured and monitored. Not-for-profits must still charge enough to make a profit but much of that profit is then reinvested in maintenance, infrastructure improvement and reserves. For-profits invest in maintenance, infrastructure and reserves as well, but they must also pay dividends or create an alternative type of financial return for investors. The bottom line is that whether hospitals or health plans are for-profit or not-for-profit, they are all motivated to make money.

Doctors are "for-profit"
One of the important points in understanding the flow of dollars through the system is that in the United States doctors—just like many other parts of the healthcare system—are for-profit. Given the enormous cost of medical school and the resulting loans, combined with significant operating expenses such as office rent, equipment costs, administrative and nursing staff payroll, and medical malpractice insurance expenses, doctors in private practice must charge enough to cover their costs and, they hope, end up with sufficient income to

facilitate a lifestyle commensurate with the amount of time, effort and money they have invested in their careers. Some doctors can choose to practice as salaried employees in a number of organizations, but these organizations must cover the same types of costs.

And just how do you value the time, effort and experience of a physician? As I mentioned earlier, it's pretty difficult to negotiate value when you are lying naked beneath a paper gown, worried about your impending diagnosis. As consumers, we get an assist from academic medical programs that establish selection mechanisms for medical school graduates to pursue different types of residencies in general and specialized medicine. Medical schools, academic medical centers and teaching hospitals work together to rigorously evaluate candidates and institutional teaching capability, essentially driving a self-regulated supply-and-demand matching system within the medical profession. Other than the tendency of the system to undervalue the general practitioner or primary care physician and the enormous cost burden thrust upon most medical school students, it works pretty well. It is from this classification of generalists and specialists that the entire area of pricing and reimbursement flows. Health plans take their cue from the physician community itself in terms of the relative value of services provided by different types of doctors. Let's see how this works from the perspective of the physician.

How providers see the healthcare pie

Physicians viewing the health plan distribution pie shown earlier might agree with it intellectually but would probably start turning red and possibly require medical assistance themselves if you were to say that only 11 percent of the healthcare dollar is spent on administration. For them, the notion that 86 percent of the dollar is reimbursement for medical care is a fallacy. That is because out of that 86 percent, hospitals, diagnostic centers, physicians, pharmacies and other suppliers have administrative costs of their own. They have to verify eligibility, submit claims, "argue" with the insurance company when services aren't authorized or claims aren't paid the way they believe they should be, figure out what the patient owes, send out statements and chase down collections from patients, and maintain proper credentials to be eligible for reimbursement. And by the way, running a business was not part of their medical school training, so there are numerous entities that "assist" physicians by doing some or all of these functions in exchange for a percentage of the medical billings. Doctors also need to pursue continuing professional education, build practices, and adapt to changing expectations from patients and health plans regarding on-line and telephonic accessibility. Many find that by forming groups or by becoming employees of an integrated delivery system or hospital, they can spend more time practicing medicine.

Hospitals, which generally have both professional management and the scale to deal with the administrative issues, are also challenged to be reimbursed properly by health plans and consumers. Both hospitals and physicians struggle just to keep track of patients, as their information systems were not originally designed to handle populations of people with unique identifiers. This ability, however, is fundamental to their being able to treat patients and collect reimbursement. And for both doctors and hospitals, the imperative that they invest heavily to implement electronic health records, and the notion that they will eventually be penalized if they do not, just adds to the perception of administrative burden.

Let the games begin
Without too much imagination, you can guess that both doctors and hospitals want to be reimbursed for their relative value to the healthcare supply chain in a manner they see as appropriate. Similarly, health plans want to price and pay for these same services in a manner they see as appropriate. And so, the basic set-up for the reimbursement game is that health plans negotiate with hospitals, doctors, pharmacies and suppliers to establish prices for their eligible health plan members—the patients and customers of these constituents. Nearly all negotiations are done based upon a series of codes, most of them indecipherable to the average healthcare consumer. There are codes for diagnoses, codes for procedures or time spent, codes for diagnostic tests, codes for drug therapies, and so forth.

It's not important that you know all the codes. What is important is that you understand what behaviors are driven by the current system. In Chapter Four, we talked about how the cost of healthcare is equal to the number of units multiplied by the price per unit. Well, there are many thousands of types of units. Some are very small and discrete, like a common blood test, and some are very large, like a heart transplant. Suffice it to say that if a lower unit cost is negotiated or a particular service is assigned a low value, some providers may be encouraged to pursue an increased number of these units in order to cover costs and achieve a desired level of income. This sets up a cat-and-mouse game and also leads to behaviors that are unfortunate for patients, such as the all-too-familiar 10-minute office visit where your doctor runs frantically from room to room so she can pay the rent.

Another place where inefficiency is rewarded by the system is in the area of medical technology. When new technology enters the marketplace there is a rush to use it. State-of-the-art imaging centers and other facilities are built to house the technology, and hospitals also invest in the new equipment. Because providers now need to pay for the expensive equipment, it is natural that they would tend to use it more. They cannot pay for it by charging higher prices for each test, because health plans have already negotiated the pricing, so providers turn to the only other way to recover their investment and stay solvent: They increase the volume of testing. Again, the incentives—not ill will or malice—drive the ordering of expensive and often unnecessary testing. In most cases, this extra testing does not harm patients. But it significantly drives up the cost of healthcare.

Paying for units produced also has consequences—albeit unintentional—in places such as hospitals, where the sicker a patient gets, the more money the hospital makes. While no one wishes to harm patients, there often is no incentive to use evidence-based protocols in order to follow best practices, thereby reducing the variation in care that so often leads to complications.

About two years ago, my administrative assistant's husband went to the hospital for a planned hip surgery. The surgery went well, in a mechanical sense, and he was out of the hospital and walking in a matter of days. Following the surgery, he developed symptoms from a serious medication-resistant infection that he had acquired at the hospital, and he was forced to return to the hospital for a several-week stay to fight the infection. This was followed by several weeks of home-based drug therapy that prevented him from returning to work. The hospital staff and doctors likely had the best of intentions as they cared for my assistant's husband; however, as he got sicker, the hospital performed more tests, billed more hospital days and, in the end, made far more money than it would have if the surgery had gone as planned.

Even under the best of circumstances, when all of the right protocols are followed, people can have bad outcomes. But it is hard to imagine that our current reimbursement structure reduces the likelihood that situations like the one I just described will occur. If the hospital had known in advance that it would be paid only for the original planned hospital stay and hip replacement procedure, would that have made the hospital more likely to follow evidence-based medicine protocols? What if we paid doctors and hospitals for the procedures they were supposed to perform in the first place and not for the care that resulted from medical error? Would my assistant's husband's hospital have taken the extra precautions necessary to reduce or eliminate the probability of acquiring a secondary infection? Better yet, what would this man's outcome have been if the financial incentives had been designed to *reward* the hospital for following these protocols and for the *quality* of his care rather than for how many procedures were performed? The terrible irony is that in spite of the higher cost of his surgery and associated tests and procedures, my assistant's husband had a worse outcome than he would have had if fewer dollars had been spent on the right things. And in fairness to the hospital in this story, is it possible that the negotiated unit cost for the hip surgery might negatively have impacted the hospital's ability to invest in the types of precautions that would have led to a better outcome—while still making a fair profit? Volume-driven medicine isn't much fun for anybody, and that is why unit pricing as a primary reimbursement methodology in many situations is probably not the best idea we can come up with. At the very least, we need to ask these questions and try to develop incentives that will encourage the best results.

There are other types of reimbursement in use today, including capitation, where a physician or physician group is paid a flat fee per patient and is responsible for delivering all of the patient's care within that budgeted amount, and episodes of care, where a physician, hospital or both in combination are paid one total price for a single condition that spans a length of time. An example of an episode of care might be where the Ob-Gyn and hospital are paid a flat rate for a patient's prenatal care through hospital discharge for a normal pregnancy and birth. Another form of reimbursement is known as per-diem, whereby a flat fee is paid for a certain level of daily care in a hospital or skilled nursing facility.

All you really need to understand is that in a system where so much more importance is placed on unit costs than on the quality or outcome of what those units produce, moving around the dollars spent in the healthcare system is much like moving the deck chairs around on the *Titanic*. Nothing will systematically change. Furthermore, if you as a consumer have no understanding of what these prices are for the relative value you are going to receive, you will be challenged to make sound, well-informed decisions. We need a better kind of pricing in healthcare, and it must be transparent so that it's not just a secret between the health plan and the doctor, the health plan and the hospital, or the health plan and the pharmacy.

Getting blame out of the way

Are you beginning to see why the average consumer could never navigate the healthcare jungle alone? Do you also understand why so many of the problems in our healthcare system have far less to do with the greed of health plans or doctors and much more to do with how the system perpetuates and rewards inefficiency?

Can you imagine if farmers, seed companies, farming- and irrigation-equipment manufacturers, and fertilizer producers spent much of their psychic and creative energy fighting with one another in pursuit of a limited dollar pool? Rather than becoming a country that has the capacity to feed much of the world by continuously improving the quality and productivity of every element in the agricultural supply chain—driving yield-per-acre to levels that were science fiction as recently as several decades ago—we might find ourselves engaged in a debate over whether too large a percentage of GDP is committed to agriculture while a disproportionate percentage of our citizens is starving.

Having married a woman whose family comes from a fertile farming region of Nebraska, I have heard the farmers at the local coffee shop complain about the government, the mega-farming corporations, the unfair business practices of the so-and-so's in the next town, and the inevitable decline of life as they knew it. Yet I have also seen the uptake of information technology in the small family farm to optimize yield while minimizing use of water and depletion of arable land, to maintain equipment to specifications that lower total cost of ownership over its useful life, and to otherwise draw upon data sources of best practices while adding personal experience and hunches. At the end of the day, the complaining is cultural but not consumptive, because everybody knows that the amount they produced for a dollar this year is just not going to be good enough next year. The fact that your family has farmed the land for a hundred years entitles you to nothing, and the allure of applying new technologies, whether seeds, equipment or chemicals, keeps the job intellectually stimulating—a constancy of learning. I have observed the same learning culture on family ranches in Wyoming and Colorado. The ubiquity of the Internet has leveled the playing field for farmers and ranchers and those who seek to supply them or distribute their production.

In polar opposition to healthcare, the agricultural industry has developed the ability to produce so much high-quality product at such a low price (even as the number of farmers has precipitously declined) that in most years the government and the industry collaborate on the level of production necessary to keep prices from being too low, essentially ensuring that the cost to consumers keeps in step with general inflation targets. Yes, there are bad years where drought or disease drives unexpected increases in costs, and good years where bumper crops exceed planning expectations, but the world does not criticize the ability of the United States to feed itself—although it might deservedly criticize what we eat.

Stop debating and start engineering

Constituents in the healthcare industry need to stop spending so much energy squaring off against each other in a zero-sum game. There needs to be an acknowledgment that we must increase healthcare "yield"—the amount of high-quality output we get for each dollar spent. We need to continuously apply our best economic discoveries at both the overall system level and the individual benefits level with our best scientific and integrated medical findings at the population and individual level to increase this "yield." Engineering healthcare to function more efficiently as a system is the only way to curb our healthcare spending. And if one wants to object philosophically to spending less on healthcare, we can spend the same but use the efficiency gains to cover the uninsured.

In order for us to become a nation of winners in the healthcare game, we have to shift our attention from policy and payment allocation to the engineering and deliberate design that will make the healthcare system do more with less money. In Chapter Eight, we'll examine how to accomplish this by bridging from the current healthcare system to a better one.

• • • • • • • • • • • • • •

Integrated Healthcare Management—the Solution

An invasion of armies can be resisted, but not an idea whose time has come.
– Victor Hugo, 'Histoire d'un crime,' 1852

It's easy to understand why many people are pessimistic about whether we can fix the U.S. healthcare system. As we have seen, healthcare is huge and complex. And rather than being intentionally designed as an effective system, it has evolved into a chaotic jungle. As a result, we have poor communication among constituents, fragmented information for you and your doctor to use in making sound decisions, and misaligned incentives that perpetuate unhealthful behaviors in consumers and unnecessary practice variation among providers—all of which have contributed to today's soaring healthcare costs. To make matters worse, the lack of an overall systematic design often causes constituents to work against one another, even while total healthcare spending in the United States continues to outpace overall economic growth. But as history has repeatedly shown, it is precisely in times of crisis that some of the best innovations are born, and healthcare is no exception. We can transform the U.S. healthcare system if we take a systems approach. The key to the solution is Integrated Healthcare Management (IHM).

Integrated Healthcare Management: sustainable affordability and quality
IHM is an approach that addresses the affordability crisis while systematically improving the quality of healthcare. It uses systematic design and information technology to share information and align incentives among healthcare constituents so they can make better choices resulting in more effective care. IHM brings together the best processes and knowledge we have for designing and administering healthcare benefits and combines those with the best processes and knowledge in care management, while tailoring this knowledge based on

the use of constituent information such as personal values and preferences. The convergence of core benefits, care management and constituent engagement areas (shown below) will provide new opportunities for consumers to become more informed, active participants in their own healthcare and will help them better partner with their providers in making key healthcare choices. This convergence zone is powered by systematic principles and information technology that create better results at lower costs. As these engagement circles converge, the IHM convergence zone grows very rapidly and opportunities for efficiency and quality improvements proliferate along with it.

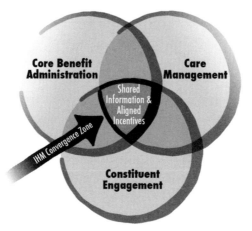

IHM will deliver better healthcare at lower cost by focusing on three straight-forward objectives:

- IHM will inform the personal choices we as consumers make about our healthcare benefit and treatment decisions along with the behaviors in which we engage, resulting in enhanced consumer access and satisfaction

- IHM will reduce unwarranted variation in care and excessive volumes of medical testing and procedures, resulting in lower medical costs and higher quality and patient safety

- IHM will engineer out administrative inefficiencies, resulting in administrative simplification

All of these objectives are currently undermined by weak communication and poor sharing of information. IHM encourages continuous improvement in health maintenance and healthcare delivery and avoids the pitfalls of merely applying price controls, which continue to misalign incentives. And because it is systematic, scalable and repeatable, IHM is not simply a bandage, but a prescription for a sustainable solution.

IHM is an especially powerful approach for several reasons. First, benefit plans will be tailored to meet the individual health needs of each consumer, as opposed to today's one-size-fits-all approach where the benefits covered and the level at which they are covered have little to do with the health status and demographics of each consumer. Secondly, healthcare information technology will knit together data about benefits coverage, treatment choices, costs, funding mechanisms (like healthcare savings accounts), and quality. Because information will no longer be locked up in silos, constituents—especially providers and consumers—will be able to collaborate more about healthcare decisions, and the huge knowledge gap between what patients understand and what their doctors comprehend about treatment choices will shrink. Information will be personalized, taking into account each patient's health status, age and life stage, economic status, personal values, and personal preferences which, as we saw earlier, can increase the likelihood that a patient will follow a doctor's instructions. Finally, IHM will enable the development of incentives that are aligned across constituents. These incentives will reward behaviors that promote the attainment of each patient's individual health goals and will discourage unwarranted variations in medical practice across the system.

IHM can be activated through a systematic, well-designed application of information technology that enables the right information to be delivered to the right constituent (person), at the right place, at the right time. In establishing an IHM approach, the following four key elements represent the underpinnings of the systems design: evidence-based medicine guidelines, aligned economic incentives (such as value-based benefits and value-based provider reimbursement), systematic health management, and active communication among constituents within a culture of health.

1. Evidence-based medicine guides IHM.
Evidence-based medicine (EBM) These care methods have been shown by scientific research to be comparatively more effective than other methods is a cornerstone of IHM. There is a large and growing body of clinical research results (i.e., evidence) from which we can derive standards for effective care

and develop new incentives. These research results come from a variety of settings, including research universities and academic medical centers, not-for-profit healthcare foundations, and for-profit health research organizations that gather and package evidence-based findings into systematic guidelines. It is true that the body of EBM guidelines and knowledge of comparative effectiveness is growing all the time, but there is plenty known today, and continuing research will just get better and better. So there is no reason for providers to delay using these important tools.

When evidence-based medicine guidelines are followed, better care is provided at a lower cost because unnecessary and ineffective care is reduced and healthy behaviors are encouraged. Let's take low-back pain as an example. Studies show that patients who participate in a physical therapy and weight-loss regimen have a similar rate of positive outcomes compared to patients who have back surgery.[13] Back surgery costs far more, and like any surgery, can put the patient at greater risk for complications. Yet many patients opt for surgery, in part because their doctors recommend it and also because patients—and in many cases, doctors—do not have up-to-date information on the outcomes of various treatment options. However, it is systematically logical that patients should not have to endure unnecessary pain and inconvenience without first actively pursuing less-invasive measures.

As I can personally attest, the decision to have surgery can sometimes lead to more care due to unexpected complications. Keep in mind that the low-back pain example is only one of many that show how lack of information about evidence-based medicine can lead to expensive decisions and questionable outcomes. In my own case, following seven surgeries, three of which were performed to correct complications or errors from prior surgeries, my doctors and I learned that my strict adherence to medication, diet, and exercise regimen are the major determining factors in keeping me out of the emergency room and preventing additional expensive medical procedures. The IHM approach ensures that providers and consumers have relevant information about evidence-based medicine before important, costly decisions are made.

2. Aligned economic incentives
Value-based benefits and value-based provider reimbursement

How do your actions as a healthcare consumer affect your own cost of health-care? And if you have health insurance already, why do you care? It is easy to think your actions have no bearing on your cost if you have health insurance. However, while in the short term most of your care may be covered, over time your choices affect not only your out-of-pocket costs but also your overall health status. It's not just big choices (as in the low-back pain surgery example) that impact the cost of healthcare, but everyday decisions as well. How much you exercise, what you eat for breakfast, lunch and dinner, and your daily hygiene habits all can affect your likelihood of developing serious and costly diseases like Type 2 diabetes and heart disease.

However, in today's system there is often little connection between the choices consumers make and how much they pay for healthcare. Also, most benefit designs today do not systematically target specific goals for each consumer, and you have few financial incentives to engage in behaviors that keep you healthy, prevent the onset of disease, and encourage you to manage diseases you may already have. In today's system, your insurance premium amount is the same whether you follow evidence-based guidelines for weight and exercise or spend your days on the couch eating doughnuts.

> *Value-based benefits remove barriers for preventive and effective patient care and provide incentives and rewards to the consumer for making the right choices, while discouraging procedures proven ineffective or dangerous.*

To help consumers more actively engage in their healthcare decisions, IHM applies *value-based benefits*—benefits designed to encourage consumers to make choices that scientifically have been shown to lead to healthier outcomes. In other words, in the world according to IHM, coverage will be customized according to each consumer's particular health profile, whether the consumer is healthy, suffers from multiple late-stage chronic conditions or falls somewhere in between. Consumers will receive a variety of financial incentives for making choices that move them closer toward meeting specific healthcare goals and for engaging in behaviors that follow evidence-based medicine. Again, the purpose of this kind of benefit coverage is to remove barriers to preventive and effective care, provide incentives and rewards for progress, and discourage bad choices.

The connection between cost and behavior change is vital. When I traveled around speaking to nearly 2,000 employees at our various offices last year, I asked the question, "Why don't you purposely drive your car into a tree?" It probably seemed like a ridiculous question because the primary answer seemed so obvious. However, the first answer I got most frequently was, "Because my car insurance premium would go up," followed by "Because I could get hurt or killed." My employees' response could not have been more effective in making my point. Somehow, the auto insurance industry has taught consumers that even though you cannot avoid all accidents, there is a financial incentive for you to try. However, consumers have not made the equivalent connection regarding their behaviors and their health—in part because health insurance today gives you no incentive to behave in a healthful way.

When a person with risk factors such as high cholesterol, high blood pressure, obesity, or any combination thereof opts not to follow the daily exercise recommended by his doctor, chooses fatty over lean meats or fruits and vegetables, and empties the salt shaker onto his food each night, he is figuratively driving his body into a tree. However, although he risks getting hurt, his behavior currently does not lead to any financial consequence. While it's a free country and people should have the right to choose their own behaviors, our nation would be systematically well served if health behaviors were associated with financial incentives designed to bring about the changes that would reduce waste and improve health. Equally important is that consumers be given the tools to understand the financial implications of each behavior and receive help keeping their bodies "on the road."

Value-based benefits are not a new concept but are just now becoming familiar to the average consumer. Many of our nation's largest employers are driving the design of value-based benefits to reduce costs while increasing adherence to evidence-based medicine. There are two types of value-based benefits: "carrots" and "sticks." The carrots are rewards in the form of low costs, discounts, cash and other positive incentives for making decisions that follow guidelines for effective care, including preventive care, patient education programs, and healthy behaviors such as working out at the gym. These carrots also include health plans waiving co-pays for preventive drugs or therapies that, according to EBM, have been shown to help patients maintain a better health status and reduce costs. Some examples of this type of preventive care for which the co-pay might be waived are asthma inhalers, cholesterol-lowering drugs, or beta-blockers following a heart attack.

The "sticks" are financial penalties or higher costs for care that does not follow guidelines for evidence-based medicine. Value-based benefits give you choices but there are different out-of-pocket price tags attached to each option. In the case of low-back pain, you can choose from various treatment options, but choosing the surgery will cost you more (particularly if you don't attempt less-invasive approaches first) because it has not been shown scientifically to be more effective than less-expensive options.

Value-based provider reimbursement: encouraging more effective ways to deliver care

Just as value-based benefits encourage responsibility for *consumption* (on the part of the consumer), value-based provider reimbursement encourages accountability for *quality production* (on the part of the provider).

Value-based reimbursement rewards physicians for taking a broader, more active role in the management of patient health and pays them for results and quality instead of solely for specific visits or procedures. Because quality outcomes often are hard to define in healthcare, the best proxy is following evidence-based protocols for care. As value-based reimbursement evolves, we will find better, more creative ways to ensure that physicians have the information they need to do the right things at the right time. They'll be encouraged to implement effective clinical systems and interact with health plans to get the information they need, because if they do not, their compensation will be negatively impacted. The best ways to reimburse for value will constantly change as evidence-based medicine continues to develop.

There are some examples already in the marketplace—pregnancy being one of them—where provider payment has moved from volume-based reimbursement to value-based reimbursement for entire episodes of care. Under the value-based reimbursement system, the provider in this example is paid a set fee for all of the different components of care necessary for a patient's healthy pregnancy and delivery (including doctor visits, testing based on evidence-based guidelines, patient education about nutrition and other important topics, and delivery). The incentive for providing care is linked to the health and well-being of the patient throughout the pregnancy and not to how many times the doctor sees her. Although this approach may seem obvious, it wasn't very many years ago that there were no incentives in place to ensure that checkpoints were followed.

Returning to the example of my assistant's husband in Chapter Seven, under a value-based provider reimbursement system the hospital would be paid for the hip surgery as an episode of care rather than for each test or procedure performed. Another important point about evidence-based provider reimbursement is that pricing for the intended procedure is warrantied by the hospital that performs it, and if any additional work were required, that work would become the financial responsibility of the provider.

Through value-based provider reimbursement, providers are paid for delivering care according to EBM protocols and for broader involvement in the management of patient health. Four nascent examples of value-based provider reimbursement are already emerging. The **patient-centered medical home (PCMH)** is a team-based arrangement led by a primary care physician who takes on the role of a healthcare quarterback and is reimbursed for managing a patient's care with a long-term perspective. He arranges specialty care when necessary and, rather than simply being a gatekeeper, coordinates with other doctors on the patient's team and collaborates with the patient to make sure she is making progress on her treatment plan. PCMHs emphasize prevention, access to care when patients need it, and the use of technology and information to encourage communication.

Another example of value-based provider reimbursement is paying providers for episodes of care for acute specialty care such as heart surgery. This care is often provided at **Centers of Excellence (COE)**, which are designed for diagnosing and treating such conditions as cancer, women's health issues, orthopedics, diabetes and heart and vascular disease. The COE model is relatively well known today. Under a value-based reimbursement model, these providers would be required to warranty their work. For example, a patient who had a hip replacement at an orthopedic center of excellence and later experienced complications would be readmitted up to six months out at no extra cost. Other developing value-based delivery models include on-line **"e-visits"** and **telemedicine** where providers are reimbursed for the time they spend providing care via telephone, the Internet or other communication modalities.

A more nascent concept includes reimbursing physicians for the delivery of **patient education**, which would spawn dynamic new methods of coding and reimbursement.

> *Just as value-based benefits encourage responsibility for consumption (on the part of the consumer), value-based provider reimbursement encourages accountability for high-quality production (on the part of the provider).*

If there's general agreement in the industry that paying providers solely for production is not a good practice, there is significant discussion as to how else providers should be paid. One school of thought suggests providers should be compensated for delivering good outcomes. While I support this notion for certain types of procedures or episodes of care where the measurement of an outcome is obvious, at a systematic level I am concerned that less thoughtful outcomes measures will incent providers to deviate from best practices in order to achieve a measure that may not be optimal for the consumer. For example, the pursuit of only an LDL cholesterol level may ignore other important risk factors to the detriment of the patient.

That's why I believe we should pay doctors for following evidence-based medicine guidelines—not solely for the results of procedures. Even if providers follow every guideline to the letter, people can still get sicker or even die. Similarly, there are some cases where providers work with anecdotal evidence and do not follow evidence-based medicine guidelines but the patient ends up with a positive result nonetheless. From a systems design and continuous quality improvement perspective, we are far better off encouraging providers to follow what we know to be the best guidelines available even if they don't lead to positive results 100 percent of the time. The alternative—incenting providers to hit an outcome target without following best practices—is a far less certain proposition. Going back to Chapter Three, The Lexus and the Human, it is important to understand that although defects and problems are bound to occur even in a best-of-class process, they are solved more quickly when they can be studied in the context of a repeatable process. This is true of manufacturing, software development and the practice of medicine.

Another caveat about value-based provider reimbursement (and IHM in general) is that it is not intended to create "sticks" for doctors in emergency rooms. When trauma cases and other situations requiring real emergency care burst through the ER doors, this is not the time for ER doctors to focus on how they will be reimbursed. Because they constantly must triage patients, emergency rooms tend to have very good standardized procedures. It is important to realize that although this type of care may be the most likely to make headlines and be featured on prime-time television, true emergency care accounts for only a small percentage of all of the care provided. IHM is designed to drive systematic improvement of the majority of care provided every day.

3. Systematic health management

In today's world, our healthcare system focuses on the management of a very small percentage of very sick people. *Systematic health management* is about proactively looking across populations of people—from the healthy to the chronically ill—to help healthy people stay healthy, sick people not get sicker, and patients along the entire spectrum improve their health status. Systematic health management includes identifying and segmenting people into groups according to their health needs, developing a health improvement plan or patient "itinerary," and monitoring progress over time to ensure that health goals are met.

With the current national focus on electronic medical records, a brief discussion of healthcare information technology is warranted. In order for electronic records to be most useful in achieving systematic health management, they must be incorporated into an overall workflow process that recognizes the benefits available to a consumer, the consumer's accessible provider network, his health history or personal health record, the incentives for physicians and consumers, and of course, the recommended care protocols. In other words, just because a medical record is in electronic form does not mean it will contribute significantly to achieving systematic health management.

For systematic health management to work effectively, providers, particularly primary care physicians, must also have their own version of their patients' health improvement plan. This plan gives providers a more holistic view of their patients' healthcare needs and goals, which will encourage a broader dialogue about overall health status, prevention and recommended treatment options when their patients are sick. Ideally, the provider's version of the health improvement plan would coordinate and be aligned with the patient's, so that when doctors follow EBM guidelines they would be rewarded financially according to value-based provider reimbursements. In the same way, patients would be rewarded via value-based benefits for making progress on their health improvement plans.

4. Constituent engagement within a "culture of health"

IHM promotes the active *engagement* of all constituents within a *culture of health*. In the IHM world, information is shared and incentives are aligned across constituents. IHM leverages technology to deliver the tools and information constituents need in order to interact effectively with one another and with the health plan. To be effective, information needs to be delivered at the right place, at the right time, in the right way, and must be accessible and transparent across constituents. As constituents work together within this culture of health, each of their roles and responsibilities will change.

• •

The Constituents' Changing Roles

Consumers like you and me will take on greater personal responsibility for choosing the plan that best meets our health needs within our financial constraints and for making good decisions when we need care. We will need to add healthcare to our list of budget items and learn about the various tools for saving for our healthcare expenses, as we will explain further in Chapter Ten.

Providers will assume broader responsibility for managing patient health, not just for the very sick but also for healthy patients. To this end, providers will develop their understanding of evidence-based medicine and recommend EBM treatment options as a means of avoiding unnecessary and ineffective care while improving the health of their patients.

Employers will help their employees to become more savvy as healthcare consumers and to learn how the decisions they make can lead to better health and lower costs. They will also promote workplace wellness, prevention and safety and increase awareness in these areas.

Brokers will facilitate collaboration between the employer and the health plan to drive employee behavior change toward healthier lifestyles.

• •

Sarah's story: IHM in action

To understand how the key elements of IHM work, let's experience a day in the life of a typical consumer in the IHM world who we'll call "Sarah." Sarah is about to sign up for health coverage. She is a 40-year-old healthy professional who, like many of us, sometimes forgets to keep up-to-date with routine screenings (like mammograms) and doesn't always make time to exercise. Sarah's daughter has difficulty keeping her asthma under control. Sarah's husband struggles with his weight and experiences low-back pain. Although Sarah has noticed that her employer's health benefits have changed markedly over the past couple of years because of rising healthcare costs, she doesn't realize how her own personal choices affect those costs. Let's follow Sarah as she experiences each step in the lifecycle and experiences the link between cost and healthy behavior in an IHM world.

Sarah's health plan guided her to the right plan.

Selecting and enrolling in a benefits plan

This year, Sarah's company's open enrollment period begins somewhat differently than in years past. Her company's benefits representative holds a meeting to explain the connection between personal choices and the cost of healthcare. He also describes a new plan that will reward Sarah and her family for making healthy choices in diet and exercise, and for complying with directions from their doctors. He explains that the plan will be tailored to Sarah and her family's specific healthcare needs, with lower out-of-pocket payments for preventive care and other care they need to stay healthy, in exchange for higher costs for elective procedures and care that is deemed "unnecessary."

Before Sarah enrolls, her health plan sends her a family health profile based on her family's previous interactions with the healthcare system and on information she has voluntarily provided (e.g., her preference to receive notifications via e-mail). The profile describes her family's health status and includes a personalized health improvement plan, or health "itinerary." This health itinerary includes information about each family member, their particular health concerns (such as her husband's being overweight according to established guidelines), the potential risks for not acting on these health concerns (such as the possibility that Sarah's husband could develop diabetes or coronary

Sarah interacts with her plan in new ways to optimize her health.

artery disease because he is overweight), and the financial incentives Sarah and her family will have in their new benefit plan to encourage healthy behaviors.

During the enrollment process, the health plan guides Sarah and her family toward a benefits plan that is the best fit for their specific needs. She learns that her plan encourages adherence to industry best practices for managing chronic diseases like asthma and, because her

Committing to health helped Sarah's whole family save money.

daughter has asthma, her plan includes 100-percent coverage for asthma-related prescriptions and services. It also includes 100-percent coverage for Sarah's yearly mammogram. Her employer's benefits plans in previous years did not completely pay for these services so Sarah either paid out-of-pocket or tried to go a little longer without them.

Staying healthy

In the past, Sarah didn't think about her health plan unless someone needed care or she had a question about her benefits. But the health improvement plan she committed to as a part of her new benefits provides a mechanism for tracking progress toward her family's health goals on an ongoing basis—not just when they are sick. Best of all, her plan rewards her family when they make healthy choices or achieve key plan milestones. For example if her husband completes his first month of a new exercise program at the local gym he'll received a $50 incentive. Also, from time to time, Sarah receives helpful reminders about ways her family can save money. To Sarah's surprise, her monthly statement shows she is paying less in monthly premiums because she and her family are achieving their health goals.

Sarah's family health coach, assigned to them by her health plan, has access to all the relevant information about her family's health status and provides support to Sarah and her family to help them stay on track with their health improvement plans. The health coach not only provides quick and relevant answers to Sarah's questions, but also suggests ways her family can save money.

For example, by switching medication brands for asthma medication, Sarah was able to reduce her prescription costs.

Accessing care

When Sarah's husband needed treatment for his back pain, his experience was dramatically different than in the past. To begin with, his doctor had access to his electronic health record and his health improvement plan. During the consultation, his doctor reviewed the treatment options with him, which included seeing an orthopedic specialist for surgery or using pain medication and exercise to address the root cause of his back pain—his weight.

Sarah's husband agreed to continue with the weight loss and financial management goals outlined in his health improvement plan. There was even a tool to help make sure he understood his options. His doctor electronically prescribed a pain medication and was able to save him $20 on the medication. Before leaving the doctor's office, Sarah's husband agreed to pay the $100 amount owed for the visit. He had received an estimate for this amount in advance so he knew how he would have to pay. Shortly after his visit, Sarah's husband received a follow-up e-mail that included a note from his doctor along with some additional information about back pain management. And they discussed his progress during a scheduled Web visit. Sarah's husband also receives, via his cell phone, regular reminders to refill his pain medication.

Over the course of the year, Sarah's health plan works together with her and her family's providers to assess how each family member is progressing toward the destinations on their healthcare itinerary or health improvement plan.

Seeking assistance with questions

Sarah used to dread calling her health plan with questions because the customer service staff often did not know the answers to her specific questions. But things are different now because the customer service department has information about Sarah's health improvement plan, her funding sources, and other relevant information, and seems to welcome the opportunity to interact with Sarah. For example, when Sarah calls her health plan about a benefit question, the customer service representatives access her records and remind her to schedule her annual mammogram. Sometimes they even send a follow-up e-mail alert about opportunities for her to save money. Sarah spends a lot of time outside her house so she prefers cell phone text messages as a way to get reminders about filling a prescription. Sarah's health plan tries to give her and her family information in the ways they prefer rather than in a mass mailing or generic communication to all of its members.

When Sarah looks back at her healthcare experience over the past year, she feels more confident about her more active role. She is relieved that her benefits plan now covers the care her family most needs such as proven asthma therapy and supplies. Because her daughter's asthma is under control, Sarah misses fewer days from work. Sarah and her husband are pleased with decisions they have made about his back pain treatment. And with the help of his health coach, doctor and on-line tools, his back is improving and he even received $100 in cash for achieving his weight-loss goal. Sarah no longer dreads calling her health plan with questions because not only do the staff answer her specific benefit, care and financial questions but they also direct her to on-line information and send her reminders and alerts that are personalized to her family's needs and health improvement goals. Above all, Sarah feels that the good healthcare decisions she and her family have made have resulted in savings and better health.

Information technology powers industry transformation

Taking a systems approach to solving the healthcare crisis cannot be done with paper and telephones; rather, must embrace the tools of this powerful age of information. Technology will enable change in healthcare just as it helped Japanese automakers transform their manufacturing and distribution processes. Technology can be used to break down the information silos that exist today to deliver comprehensive, useful information to constituents at the right place, at the right time and in the most helpful way. As a result, a greater degree of transparency—complete information that is shared among constituents—will be achieved. Transparency is most obvious in pricing. If consumers and providers have the same understanding about how much of the cost of care will be paid by the consumer and how much will be paid by the health plan, the provider can collect payment from the consumer right at the time of the appointment. Another example of transparency is the health improvement plan that the doctor and the health plan will develop for each consumer based on evidence-based medicine guidelines. For example, if a patient has Type 2 Diabetes, both he and his doctor would have the same understanding of what the patient's dietary restrictions are and how often he should check his glucose level. This transparency will allow patients and doctors to work toward the same goal and to talk about behaviors that deviate from evidence-based medicine guidelines.

Technology will also enable the long-awaited implementation of personal health records (described in greater detail in Chapter Nine). In addition, many other creative applications of technology will help equip consumers to more actively engage in their healthcare decisions.

How IHM will save money

We just saw how Sarah and her family reduced their healthcare costs while also improving their health. Would it surprise you to learn that if Integrated Healthcare Management were to be implemented across the U.S. population, we could knock 20 percent to 25 percent off the total cost of healthcare? Field studies[14] using actual claims and experience data from U.S. health plans show that the application of even basic IHM principles can result in savings of 10 percent of total commercial medical costs. If you extrapolate this number over 151 million employer-sponsored beneficiaries, it would result in projected savings of $72.7 billion. The savings come from the following major categories:

- Three percent of the savings come from consumer-focused programs targeting wellness, health improvement and education

- 33 percent of the savings come from consumer-focused programs targeting informed decision-making and improved treatment compliance that are reinforced through value-based benefits

- 35 percent of the savings come from decreased provider practice variation and a move to evidence-based medicine through electronic health records and value-based reimbursement

- 29 percent of the savings come from increased provider focus on treatment management and care coordination for patients with more complex conditions

The greatest savings opportunities in IHM come from consumers who have multiple late-stage conditions.

Who can lead the way to IHM?

IHM is not an exclusionary systematic design. It provides a framework for consumers, providers, employers, brokers and health plans to get on the same page. As we saw in Chapter Seven, healthcare is currently a politically charged zero-sum game. Consequently, much energy is expended debating the motivation of health plans and providers or the trust (or lack thereof) that consumers have in different parts of the system. This debate is irresolvable, and it just encourages constituents and policymakers to take pot shots at one another. Systematically, consumers regard information they receive from their doctor (regardless of its original source) as most reliable. This perception will be even stronger when the consumer and the doctor are both on the same page thanks to value-based benefits, value-based provider reimbursements, evidence-based medicine, and systematic health management.

In general, entities that touch the most parts of the healthcare elephant are best suited to be able to design benefits, design reimbursements, set up high-level systematic care plans and automate evidence-based medicine into workflow. Based upon that assertion, health plans and integrated delivery systems are best positioned to take on this role. Individual providers or even providers loosely affiliated around a hospital are unlikely to be able to achieve the required level of coordination on behalf of the consumer. Also regardless of how health plans may be viewed, A survey conducted by TNS for The TriZetto Group in late 2007 showed that constituents in aggregate believe that health plans are the entities with the best baseline information capabilities to put IHM in motion. (Remember, both benefits and care must be coordinated in an optimal way to get the best quality of healthcare for each dollar spent and achieve IHM.)

In addition, health plans already have data about interactions among consumers and providers as well as detailed benefit information—all of which would serve as the foundation for this new approach. As we saw in Chapter Seven, through automation and other technological advances, health plans have made great strides in reducing the portion of the healthcare dollar that is spent on benefit administration. Health plans' facility with technology and their position at the center of the healthcare supply chain will enable them to add continuous value for consumers, providers, employers, and brokers to improve care and reduce cost.

Making the jump from the healthcare jungle to IHM

As you can see, Integrated Healthcare Management has the potential to transform the U.S. healthcare system, reducing skyrocketing costs and improving quality of care.

And just as the roles and responsibilities of the other healthcare constituents will change with the IHM approach, so too will the role of the health plan. While health plans are positioned well in the supply chain to drive change, they will have to make some significant changes themselves in order for IHM to succeed. Health plans will have to shift their role from that of claims processor to one of health and wellness facilitator. They will need to focus on whole-person care—becoming a patient's advocate over time and across medical conditions—rather than simply collecting premiums and paying out claims for care in the short term. Health plans will have to create a culture of health in which they encourage each constituent to do a better job of following the steps that lead to better health and adherence to evidence-based medicine.

While health plans will manage the distribution of information, create aligned incentives, continuously monitor how well consumers are doing in meeting their healthcare goals, and provide support to consumers and other constituents, they will not in any way be regarded as a substitute for highly trained physicians. In the IHM world, health plans will drive the system and help each element of the healthcare system interact more smoothly and effectively; however, physicians will maintain their sacred role in providing care to patients. My hope is that by using the IHM approach, the adversarial relationship between health plans and providers that has existed historically will give way to an era where health plans empower physicians as the quarterbacks of systematic healthcare management.

EHRs, PHRs, EMRs—what are these confusing acronyms? And why are they such a central part of the current healthcare debate? In Chapter Nine, we will take a look at these repositories of patient health information, how they can reduce waste and decrease the number of medical errors, and how PHRs can be implemented much sooner than the time lines discussed on Capitol Hill.

• • • • • • • • • • • • • •

Digital Alphabet Soup: Understanding EHRs, EMRs and PHRs

What's in a name? That which we call a rose
By any other name would smell as sweet.
– William Shakespeare

The use of healthcare information technology to improve U.S. healthcare is front and center in our national healthcare reform debate. In the popular press, healthcare information technology has become synonymous with the concept of electronic health records (EHRs). Moreover, many people believe that if health records can be computerized (digitized) and shared (with appropriate security), they will help solve both cost and quality problems in healthcare. It's interesting to note that because the federal government has indicated that large sums of money will be allotted to promote the adoption of EHRs, nearly every major technology company, and every other company remotely associated with healthcare suddenly has an EHR solution that is worthy of consideration and reimbursement. I'm reminded of the explosive hype around the initial development of the Internet in the late 1990s, and how even though massive capital was applied to unlock the usefulness of the Internet communications channel, only a small handful of companies developed solution models that survive today.

The fact is, while electronic records will be a key component of improving the U.S. healthcare system, the implementation of a meaningful, sustainable solution requires a combination of people (that is, the constituents we discussed in Chapter Five), processes, *and* technology. And having read the book to this point, you likely understand that if you try to solve a specific problem only by implementing technology, even if that technology is very advanced, it is still simply an applied technology (e.g., the use of EHRs to reduce the chance of medication errors). In order to change things in a coordinated, systematic way, we must incorporate applied technologies as pieces of an overall design that considers all requirements of the system. Improving healthcare through Integrated Healthcare Management is a perfect example. Because we know that IHM is intended to optimize both benefits and care for the consumer, we must incorporate the EHR as part of a broader enterprise framework that promotes value-based benefits, value-based reimbursement, systematic health management and evidence-based medicine guidelines within a culture of health.

Certainly, this is a tall order, and our nation will not get there overnight. Therefore, sensible steps that create the energy and will to move our industry in this direction, such as the current attention being given to EHRs by President Barack Obama, will help fuel progress. However, even for the typical consumer, not to mention health professionals and policymakers, it is important to understand what we are seeking if we are to meet or exceed expectations regarding the promise of electronic health records. President John F. Kennedy's goal of reaching the Moon was systematically far less complicated than today's call to provide accessible affordable and quality healthcare for all Americans.

This chapter will discuss both the promise and misconceptions of the use of EHRs and will make a strong case for how one "flavor" of EHR, known as the personal health record (PHR), can be applied immediately and relatively inexpensively to move us toward the promise of Integrated Healthcare Management while complementing initiatives underway in hospitals and physician offices.

First, let's clarify the alphabet soup of EHRs, EMRs and PHRs being discussed with regard to health records. These acronyms refer to just three of the many different types of health records either in use today or that are being developed, and many people are confused as to which is which. *"Electronic health record (EHR)"* is the term you see in the news most often, as it has become the subject of government healthcare reform, and has therefore entered the public lexicon. *Electronic medical records (EMRs)*, which are used primarily in hospital settings, are hospital visit-specific, and are in fairly widespread use today, particularly in integrated delivery systems. *Personal health records (PHRs)* typically are designed to be used by both consumers and providers. Like EHRs and EMRs, PHRs are being implemented and adopted at various rates across the country. Yet by their very nature, PHRs offer an opportunity to accelerate the progress toward Integrated Healthcare Management.

A closer look at EMRs, EHRs and PHRs.

EMRs: Electronic records—usually hospital/clinic-centered
Characteristics:

- *Depth of content: Very deep*

- *Designed for use by: Specialized clinicians*

- *How widely they are used: Relatively narrowly—affiliated buildings, campuses, and remote medical offices*

- *Time span of included information: Short—based around current episode of care*

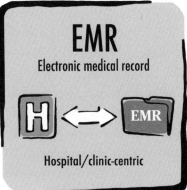

In the hospital and advanced clinical setting, which can be very complex, the electronic record system (the EMR) needs to provide all the vital data about patients, no matter where they go within the hospital—from the surgical theater to the MRI machine to the hospital room. The hospital record contains clinical data geared to the expertise level of the treating physicians and nurses throughout the hospital, including numerous specialists. The EMR typically is designed to highlight data for one relatively contained episode of care in one particular hospital organization. In some cases, the record also includes or can enable treating physicians to access historical data from specific treatment centers and practices that are affiliated with the hospital in which the patient is being treated.

The EMR is a deep record in that it contains a tremendous amount of detail, potentially including data-intensive lab results, patient readings and X-rays, EKGs or other diagnostic images used in determining or adjusting treatment at any point in time or location within the hospital. The format of the EMR is designed to be understood by healthcare professionals, not everyday consumers like you and me, nor is it intended to be distributed outside that narrow clinical setting. Improving patient safety during a hospital visit is a vitally important goal of hospital-based electronic medical records. Many hospital care processes (or workflows) differ widely from those in other healthcare settings—and even from other hospitals. Therefore, patient data must be updated very quickly, as hospitalized patients are often in life-threatening or acute situations.

In reality, even within a single institution, today's hospital-based EMRs are still evolving from separate systems operating in narrow silos, toward a more integrated tool that creates more value for all constituents. For example, many hospitals still have multiple departmental EMRs within their four walls. It is not uncommon to find separate systems storing data for radiology, pathology and other key hospital functions. Often, caregivers must log on to each of these systems separately and connect the dots themselves when making healthcare decisions. And recall from Chapter Four that many physicians in most hospitals also are part of private practices (which may use other types of health records). While today's EMR is far from an ideal systematic and integrated record system, it is vitally important in enabling complex care settings to function safely and efficiently. Over time, as more hospitals come on-line with such important tools, the detailed clinical data can be integrated with other healthcare information systems at physicians' offices and health plans in support of health consumers (in this case, patients receiving care in a hospital). Adding to the systematic complexity of EMRs, once monolithic general hospitals throughout the country are re-making themselves into a hybrid of centers of excellence and coordinated care entities, which means still further types of workflows and processes will be continuously evolving.

EHRs: Electronic records in physician offices
Characteristics:

- *Depth of content: Deep*

- *Designed for use by: General clinicians, specialists and nurses*

- *How widely they are used: Very narrowly—usually only offices affiliated with that practice*

- *Time span of included information: Length of time patient is seen by that practice*

Information needs and care processes in the doctor's office are often very different from those in the hospital. As we've discussed, physicians practice in a variety of setting types, ranging from one- and two-person practices to very large integrated delivery systems with outpatient facilities such as Kaiser or the Veterans Administration (VA). Because of the diversity of size, complexity and resource support (for example, a rural doctor likely has no dedicated IT staff) the information needs differ among physicians. Physician practice electronic health records can be as simple as turning paper charts into electronic documents for easy retrieval. More advanced record systems integrate multiple physician office functions, such as medical records, order entry, results reporting, appointment scheduling, and insurance and patient billing. These advanced, integrated EHR systems are especially useful for multi-specialty group practices where primary care physicians and specialists coordinate care among themselves, as well as with their on-site lab and pharmacy. A recent study published in *The New England Journal of Medicine* estimated that less than 17 percent of physicians have adopted any type of EHR, and less than 4 percent have adopted the more advanced, integrated form.[15]

In contrast to the hospital-based record, the practice-based electronic health record is designed to give the doctor a longer-term view of the patient, usually the length of the relationship between the patient and physician. Patients receiving treatment in the office setting typically have less critical conditions than those receiving treatment in the hospital. For example, they may go to their doctor's office for routine examinations or for ongoing treatment for chronic conditions. However, all of these scenarios require care management over a much longer period of time than for an acute care hospital situation. Record systems in physician practices also are designed for use by a more limited number of staff who tend to be familiar with one another, and many of whom deal with less day-to-day clinical intensity than their hospital counterparts.

Some healthcare advocates have suggested that physician-based EHRs become transportable and shareable across the healthcare supply chain to eliminate errors and redundancy. Systematically, one needs to consider whether using records in that manner is congruent with physicians' objectives for their own record systems and workflow. It should be pretty easy to understand that the workflow in an orthopedic specialist's office is (and should remain) very different from that of an oncologist or a primary care physician. And so, the acceptable middle ground is the creation of standardized data sets within differing EMR systems, so that each type of record solution can draw in the data and present it in a format that is familiar to the clinician viewing it. There is a significant amount of work to be done in the advancement of EMRs based in physician-offices, because from a practical perspective, EMRs ultimately must produce both improved quality and efficiency (i.e., better results without reducing throughput)—not just additional overhead.

PHRs: Electronic records across physician offices, hospitals and other caregivers

Characteristics:

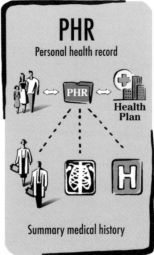

- *Depth of content: Shallow but broad*

- *Designed for use by: Many, from consumer to provider to other caregivers*

- *How widely they are used: Broadly—With permission, accessible to all who need it*

- *Time span of included information: Very long—segmented by year*

The third type of electronic health record is the personal health record (PHR). There are many variations of this type of record. These range from the do-it-yourself variety, where consumers enter data about their health history and care, to record systems in which the key data is automatically fed from other data sets in the healthcare system (for example, by a health plan). Because they are Internet-based, PHRs can be viewed from any location and, in compliance with security and privacy protections, can be seen by anyone who is required to see them.

What all PHRs have in common is their summary nature and unique ability to be used universally. The simplest way to think about a PHR is as an outline of your healthcare history, or your health résumé. Certain types of PHRs provide a comprehensive view of the patient, which currently is not available from any other type of record. Unlike today's hospital- and physician-based medical records, which contain information only from affiliated locations (at best), the PHR can provide a comprehensive overview of all diagnoses, procedures, testing and treatments, across all locations and practitioners. The PHR does not necessarily contain specific test results or detailed notes on treatment (although it can); rather, it lists the types of tests performed, their dates, and the names of the providers by whom they were ordered and performed. This summary-level information can act as a prompt for doctors to get more detailed information if necessary. It is easy to see how the PHR's breadth helps physicians and others throughout the healthcare supply chain identify potential drug interactions, avoid duplicate testing, make comparative evaluations and cross-check the care you are receiving across all your treatment centers.

Another important advantage of the PHR is that it can be understood easily by consumers and providers alike. All of the physicians, nurses, and therapists involved in your care (and even your own family members, with your permission) are capable of using it. Because it is in summary form, the PHR is useful in a wide variety of settings, including the home, the doctor's office, and when a patient first arrives at a hospital for treatment.

One size doesn't fit all

In Chapter Four we saw that big-box supply chain organizers such as Walmart utilize enterprise information to create high efficiency within their four walls. We learned that Amazon uses information technology to create a *virtual* supply chain for consumers that is not dependent upon physical location. Just as retailers use different models for organizing and managing supply chains, the U.S. healthcare system's varied and expanding range of delivery models will likely require differing electronic health record solutions to handle the full range of healthcare benefits and delivery methods across the system. Simply put, a one-size-fits-all approach to clinical electronic health records will not deliver the system-wide cost, quality and access improvements we seek.

Having been behind the firewalls and in the shoes of many different healthcare constituents, I can personally attest to the need for multiple health record models that are integrated with one another. I was involved in the implementation of the earliest electronic medical records and physician records in integrated delivery networks; I've been a patient on the receiving end (both good and bad) of the information in these records; I have accompanied primary and specialty physicians going about their daily work; and as a board member of a hospital I maintain familiarity with current health record implementation initiatives. Given the wide spectrum of information needs across healthcare constituents and the differences in how their workflows and computer systems are designed, it is clear that we will need to employ multiple types of records but we must also make sure they are linked and coordinated appropriately within the construct of Integrated Healthcare Management. We cannot lose sight of the ultimate objective of health record systems: better coordination of benefits and care at the right time and place in the consumer (patient) and provider interaction.

The dream—national and regional health information networks and exceptions

If you step back from the complexity I just described, it is probably easy to see why many people who do not have a detailed understanding of the entire healthcare supply chain are lobbying hard for Regional Health Information Organizations (RHIOs), National Health Information Networks (NHINs) or Health Information Exchanges (HIEs) that bring forth the concept of interoperability of EHR, and EMR systems data from any source. The classic story used to make this case is about a person who gets into an accident while on vacation in another state and is "saved" because his medication history is instantaneously available to the emergency room physician, who is viewing the patient's health record on-line as the patient arrives. Another version explains how the chest image of a vacationing tourist is retrieved from her doctor's office across the country, allowing the patient to be diagnosed and treated rapidly, avoiding a potentially fatal aneurism. To be clear, I am in favor of such capabilities and, as a patient myself, I hope for the day when these types of stories become routine. However, much more is involved than most people think. Specifically, the base data in every doctor's office and hospital would need to be digitized; the data standards would need to be common across all different EHR and EMR solutions and locations; the exchange would need to be able to precisely identify the requestor and source of the data; and security measures would have to be designed to ensure that the requestor was authorized to see the data. While the concept of multiple record systems that can share information makes good sense, creating this apparent panacea is not as easy as it may seem. The political controversy over who administers the connected exchange of such data is why so many local, regional and national models and efforts have emerged. In fact, interoperability (as it is called in the IT world) has never existed across non-affiliated entities in any industry to the degree people are calling for in healthcare.

Looking at a few examples in industries that have fairly advanced information technology systems may help to make my point. Many people like to use banking as an example of an industry with this type of interoperability. Their rationale is that you can retrieve cash from any ATM in the world as long as you have money or credit. But this example is not truly analogous to the interoperable electronic health record examples I just described. Sending information to facilitate the transfer of cash balances among different institutions' accounts is a relatively simple transaction, like sending an electronic prescription to a pharmacy in healthcare or checking insurance eligibility—transaction already in daily use.

One analogy I can think of to suggest the level of healthcare record interoperability some seek is the following hypothetical example. Suppose you had a brokerage account at Merrill Lynch with fixed- income bonds that are *actively traded*, a brokerage account at Bank of America Securities with a portfolio of stocks that are actively traded, a checking account at Bank of America, two savings accounts at your local savings and loan, and an options and commodities *trading* account with Citigroup. Now, suppose that you want to instantly be able to look across the detailed history and current activity of all of the investments and accounts from one system, and make that information available (with proper security, of course) to any professional in any of those financial institutions. The fact is that each bank has proprietary ways of formatting and displaying data to consumers and also for internal purposes, which is why the banking industry has not reached the level of complete interoperability in the hypothetical situation described. And even though Walmart or Toyota can efficiently exchange electronic information with its suppliers, Walmart is not likely to try and "interoperate" your purchase data with Amazon or Target.

The Federal Aviation Administration (FAA) air traffic control system is another example held up as supposedly interoperable but it is actually a command-and-control system. This system has the appearance of interoperability because every airline seems to be connected despite their being completely different companies. However, this system relies instead on certain components such as continuous active transmission of electronic signals, a centrally controlled radar system, highly-trained pilots that must obey instructions from other humans (e.g., air-traffic controllers), etc.

Information technologists will almost always say—because they truly believe it—to those who seek a connected vision, that a "layer" of software (rules) can be built to make things interoperable, as long as common data standards exist. This claim may be true for static data that needs to be pulled together from disparate sources for a specific single transaction or inquiry and for defined-format electronic transactions. But once data "goes in motion," meaning it is used in a process by a person or acted upon by a set of software rules that potentially change the context (the information value) of the data, then things can easily go awry.

Does this mean we should give up on connected EHRs that can be shared among providers and consumers? Absolutely not. But we do have to take a step back from the problem to be able to solve it. From a systematic viewpoint, the first relevant question is: Around which constituent are you going to center the health record? This answer is obvious—it's the consumer. The next relevant question is: Which constituent has data containing the fullest view of the consumer? As we will see, except in the case of a single-payer situation (like the VA) or an integrated delivery system that also administers the benefits for its patients, the systematic answer to the question is payers (health plans). As you recall from Chapter Six, payers have an abundance of fully digitized benefits data that reflect the diagnoses and care received across all care settings.

Acknowledging the data accuracy debate

Let me restate, for clarity, that I am not suggesting that the payer-based PHR is a substitute or clinical equivalent to hospital-based records and records based in a physician office, but it is a powerful jump-start towards achieving the goal of patient-centered connected records. I should also mention that in the 20-plus years I have been implementing clinical and administrative information systems, I have heard the same arguments from physicians, time and time again, about "poor data quality"—that some of the data (and therefore the information produced by the data) is just plain wrong. These physicians are absolutely right! Ironically, these same physicians are often the origin (or entry source) of the data, and they know precisely what coding limitations or less-than-perfect entry processes cause the data to be wrong. For example, some physicians may want to document health information that is more specific than what is available within the coding options. For example, physicians who want to record a drug allergy may be able to find a code for an allergic reaction to a chemical class but not to a specific ingredient. However, the overarching point regarding electronic records is that while the coding process has limitations, even in the life-and-death business of healthcare data that is mostly correct or even directionally correct can add great value to the overall system, as long as you keep it in context and apply it judiciously in the workflow.

PHRs: getting there faster, cheaper and better

As of now, all types of electronic health record systems are at early stages of market adoption, even though there are notable industry leaders serving mostly larger provider and payer organizations with excellent record solutions. To accelerate the rate at which electronic records are adopted, the American Recovery and Reinvestment Act passed in February 2009 provides payment incentives for the adoption of physician practice EHRs, with an objective of moving from less than 20 percent adoption today to near ubiquity within five years. In reality, I believe achieving this important goal in clinical settings is likely to take more than a decade. But that does not mean we should delay their implementation, nor does it mean we must wait ten years or more to achieve the objective of delivering better information accurately and consistently to every patient/caregiver interaction.

To understand how we can accomplish the goal of implementing PHRs let's review some of the concepts from this book. First, take another look at the supply-chain picture below.

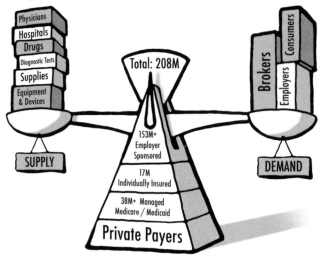

Now let's take another look at how the healthcare premium dollar is distributed (from Chapter Seven).

The Healthcare Dollar
from a Payer Perspective

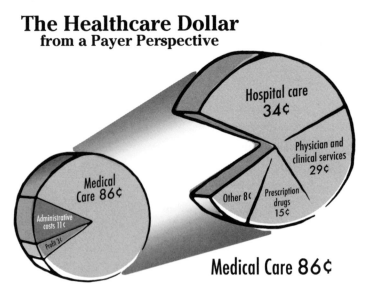

Approximation based upon data combining Medicare population and commercial data. (Source: Adapted from centers for Medicare and Medicaid Services [2007] and 2008 Combined Util SEER – Volume II C – General Edition, Comprehensive Total Summary of Medians, Sherlock Company.)

From a systematic standpoint, it should be clear that the healthcare dollar flows through the payer and is distributed to the "supply side" of the supply chain. In order to get reimbursed their portion of the dollar, the physicians, hospitals, diagnostic testing centers, and pharmacies submit "claims" to the payer, who then has a record of all this activity at the individual consumer (patient) level. This data is close to 100 percent digitized, as the industry has had electronic submission incentives for many years.

Now let's take another look at the information silos discussed in Chapter Six.

As you can see, the data contained in just the benefits silo is a rich source of information that can be used in a health record to show the health history (diagnoses and treatments) for a particular patient. The payers also have data in the other information silos that can be used to enrich electronic health records (more about that in a moment). Let's add one more illustration to show the relationship between the payer-based PHR and other data sources. Your answers to several straightforward questions will help explain this illustration.

1. In a given year, do you typically see multiple doctors in different practices?

2. In a typical year, do you receive care at multiple medical facilities (offices)?

3. Do you have diagnostic tests (e.g., blood work or imaging) at still other locations?

4. Do you get your prescriptions filled at one or more retail pharmacy locations?

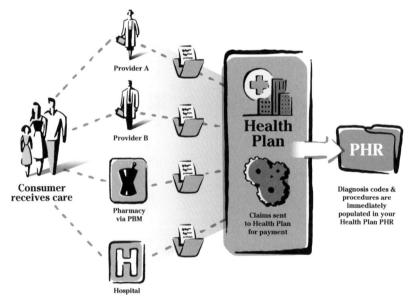

If you are a typical U.S. healthcare consumer, you answered "yes" to all four questions. If you were able to answer "no" to all four questions, then you probably receive your care in an integrated delivery system that coordinates the supply side of the supply chain on your behalf. Now let's ask a fifth question:

5. Are your health insurance benefits administered by the same overall organization that is providing you the care outlined above?

If you can answer "yes" to all five questions, then you are in a situation (probably an integrated delivery system with a directly attached benefit plan, for example Kaiser Permanente or the VA) where the organization providing your care has the ability to create a good personal health record. If you answered "no" to any of the questions (which puts you in the company of the majority of Americans), then your health plan is likely in the best position to create your PHR, because it naturally gathers digitized data from multiple doctors, hospitals, diagnostic testing centers and pharmacies, to aggregate the data on your behalf to be shared among you, your physician(s) and other caregivers. Regardless of which category you ended up in, the point is that we can and should all have PHRs. Considering that most people only have one health plan in a given year, and so much data flows through that health plan, the absence of a PHR in any case is a waste of good, digitized data.

If you have followed the logic to this point, then you should ask yourself one more important question: If I change my health plan and the claims data that makes up my health history doesn't "follow" me to my new health plan, isn't that bad? The answer is "yes." In order for PHRs to be most useful, the standardized claims and administrative data that populate them must be transportable. Much as providers have learned that sharing clinical data on behalf of patients can help improve patient care, so too have payers learned that transportable records are required in order to have an efficient industry business model. Systematically and practically, transportability is quicker and more practical than interoperability. This is because payers are accustomed to adding populations of consumers along with claims history to their information systems due to years of industry consolidation and the way this data resides in payer systems is already highly standardized.

Remember...IHM is *benefits* and *care*
The description above illustrates how all the data from nearly every significant point where we as consumers touch the healthcare system, is funneled through the health insurance payment system. This process has been in effect

for decades, as care providers throughout the healthcare delivery system submit patient encounter and claims data in order to get paid. As a result, our healthcare system already has a tremendous digitized health history data asset that can be leveraged through personal health records to start delivering better information for every patient/care interaction.

Clinical data alone from these record systems, while helpful, is not enough. The next step in building our data chain must be integrating the digitized diagnoses and treatment data with other critical data that the physician needs to fully serve a patient.

To give patients and doctors a full picture of the patient health status, clinical data must be coordinated with benefits information, as well as with information about how the patient prefers to receive information and communicate. For example, a Web-based personal health record with physician-guided content and e-mail reminders can be a great tool—except when your patient is an 85-year-old senior who doesn't often use a computer. Likewise, it's not all that useful to the patient if the doctor recommends a treatment that isn't covered by the patient's insurance and that he cannot afford on his own. Nor would the patient be well served if his doctor were to refer him to a specialist who is not part of his health plan's approved network.

In addition to being able to integrate benefits information with clinical data, a well-designed PHR should enable providers to know which communication methods each patient prefers for receiving information about her healthcare. In collecting information about these communications preferences PHRs should not rely on the assumption that all consumers have reliable access to computers. While many of us are able to enter that information on the PHR's Web site, preference information can just as easily be collected at benefits enrollment time, whether that's on-line, on paper or by phone.

It is also important that data populating PHRs be comprehensive, relevant and current. Today, providers and pharmacists are naturally incented to enter and transmit the data that leads to payment for their services as quickly as possible. Even claims that are submitted on paper are systematically digitized by health insurers, meaning that nearly 100 percent of health insurance claims data are available for PHRs. As I mentioned earlier, payer-based PHRs are no substitute for hospital-based and physician-office based record systems. In both of these cases, the healthcare activities and results may be flowing just minutes apart. A PHR is not intended to keep up with the pace of physician or office workflow, but when the visit or episode is completed, the resultant data will feed the PHR and update the consumer's health résumé

To be fully effective as a tool for caregivers and patients, summary health background information must be available anytime and anywhere. Most PHRs include the Internet as one option for viewing health records, meaning that as long as the consumer, physician (or other caregiver) has a ubiquitous Internet connection (and the proper security), he can access the record. Because they must be embedded in day-to-day (even minute-to-minute) workflows, EHRs and EMRs have different challenges in exposing a broad view of the patient across multiple and non-affiliated locations over the Internet.

Let's not forget security and privacy
Most EHR, EMR and PHR systems have strong data security safeguards, such as encryption, to prevent random hacking or unintended distribution (such as when a PC and its hard drive are stolen). However, the treatment of information privacy and control for authorized users is not so clear-cut. This topic is important for all of us as healthcare consumers. Right now, there is a debate among both advocates and developers of all types of electronic health records about privacy and who should have control over the data. Some people are advocating that, under current privacy laws, electronic health records could be shared among doctors and other treatment centers without specific permission from, or even knowledge by, the patient. Others advocate that consumers should always be in control of the distribution of all or parts of their health information, except in extreme circumstances, such as when a patient is unconscious in the emergency room. Rather than turning this debate into a battle that pits healthcare providers against consumer and privacy advocacy groups, it should be reframed in the context of supporting and understanding current Health Insurance Portability and Accountability Act (HIPAA) regulations. These regulations allow for the authorized flow of healthcare information among HIPAA entities for purposes of treating a patient, and give patients control over the sharing of information with other entities.

To a large extent, the privacy issues come down to doctor-centered versus patient-centered control. In short, it probably makes practical sense that EHRs and EMRs are more of a provider-controlled system, and that payer-based PHRs are more of a consumer-controlled system, but that both are assumed "shareable" to HIPAA entities unless these records are specifically turned off. And certainly, there is a shared understanding in the medical and payer communities that in certain situations it might make sense to require an additional level of authorization from the consumer to reveal certain behavioral health matters and other particularly sensitive diagnoses. In just one example, my company, TriZetto, has patented a process that allows consumers to grant access selectively via personal software "keys" to different levels of their personal health information. In my trips to Washington, D.C., and in my company's participation on standards committees, I find that policymakers are doing a good job of exploring the debate over consumer and provider control of healthcare data, and the issue may ultimately be determined by healthcare reform legislation.

There are two final points to understand about PHRs. First, on a relative time-and-expense-basis, PHRs largely could be in place and adopted much sooner and for a fraction of the cost of EMRs and EHRs, at least for the over 200 million people whose benefits are managed by private payers (and for fee-for-service Medicare beneficiaries as well). Second, the aggressive pursuit of PHRs will actually improve the usefulness and "interoperability" of EMRs and EHRs. This is because the claims data in the PHR contains the date-of-service, the place (location) of service and the treating physician as well as the diagnoses and treatments, essentially creating the search engine parameters to track down and connect otherwise disparate data sources.

Experiencing your personal health record in an IHM world
We'll conclude this chapter by describing an example of how the use of a payer-based PHR can optimize benefits and care for both the consumer (patient), and the doctor.

You call a new doctor's office to make an appointment. When you arrive, instead of having to fill out all the forms about who you are, what health conditions you have, what medications you take and who is your insurance carrier and emergency contact, the office already has that information. By the time you arrive at your doctor's office, the staff has sent a standard eligibility verification request to your health plan. In other words, the request confirms that you have insurance coverage for this visit. Along with the eligibility verification that is sent back to the doctor's office comes a neatly formatted copy of your health résumé, which includes not only the information from the form, but your high-level health history as well.

As a result, when the nurse is checking your blood pressure and temperature, she is able to verify that the recently filled prescriptions on your health résumé are accurate so you don't have to try to remember their names and doses. Because the nurse has accurate information about you she is probably better able to do the initial interview with you about the reason for your visit. As the doctor walks into your examination room he is already leafing through your personal health record that was printed when your eligibility was confirmed (or looking at it as an electronic document), seeing what diagnoses and treatments other doctors past and present have made, as well as medications you have been prescribed. He can see that while you came to see him about your right knee, there was an X-ray of that knee taken last year at the ski resort where you originally injured it. He seems pleased because it will give you both something to compare any new diagnostic images against, and he asks his nurse to see if that image is electronically retrievable. It turns out that that clinic that performed that diagnostic test has an EMR that can e-mail the image in a matter of minutes.

After seeing that no severe knee injury was present on the prior image, and after physically examining you, the doctor suggests an exercise and physical therapy regimen along with a prescription to reduce the pain and inflammation around your knee. He comments that without that image, he would have sent you for a CT scan or perhaps an arthroscopic procedure by an orthopedic surgeon. You comment that the time and expense of either would have been difficult on you. Later, at the instruction of the doctor, you make an appointment with the physical therapist, whom the doctor's staff has already verified is within your approved network of providers. They also "clicked" the contact information for the physical therapist into your PHR. At the time you make the appointment with the physical therapist, the front desk tells you exactly how much you will owe for this service. Behind the scenes, your insurance company already had informed the imaging center of your financial responsibility when the physical therapist's office checked your eligibility, based on a calculation that included your covered benefits (in this case, the number of physical therapy visits you are allowed) and your deductible status.

As part of your recovery and rehabilitation, the doctor requests that you log in to your health record and mark down your daily rehabilitation and exercise activities, which are based upon evidence-based protocols, for future review. At your follow-up visit, your physician can see on your health record how well you have done, as can other doctors you visit subsequently. In other words, the PHR can help the doctor see (and you track) how well you are complying with the recommended course of treatment. This provides information that enables both value-based benefits and value-based reimbursement.

Now imagine that the systems that made all this happen so smoothly were available today at no additional cost to consumers or providers. That vision is not a distant reality. It can, and is being prepared and delivered in selected regional markets through personal health records powered by health plan information. Is it the *perfect* answer? No. But it's a powerful start, and that's what is most important.

Moving ahead now

The time for the PHR is now. It presents a tremendous opportunity to improve healthcare dramatically in the near term, while the physician practice-based EHR and hospital-based EMR data become more widely implemented. Advancing PHRs at this time in no way impedes those other record systems; rather, it helps all three models grow together toward a fully integrated healthcare management system in the United States. The imperative heard often in Washington of late, from everyone all the way up to President Barack Obama, seems to best summarize the case: "When it comes to addressing our health care challenge, we can no longer let the perfect be the enemy of the essential."[16]

Now that you have seen Sarah's world in Chapter Eight and we've seen the promise of electronic health records in enhancing the dialogue and flow of information among constituents, I hope you see that our healthcare system can and will be transformed. Chapter Ten examines your changing responsibilities as a consumer of healthcare, and how society can educate you in preparation for your new role.

• • • • • • • • • • • • •

Personal Responsibility and Societal Opportunity

An individual without information cannot take responsibility; an individual who is given information cannot help but take responsibility.

– Jan Carlzon, former president and CEO of
Scandinavian Airlines System (SAS)

Now that you have accompanied me through the healthcare jungle, you have a basic familiarity with its elements, how it works, its deficiencies and areas of strength, and how the system can be designed to provide higher-quality care at a lower cost using the Integrated Healthcare Management approach. So what does all of this mean for you? Should you think differently about your role as a consumer of healthcare? By now you may be pondering whether healthcare is an inalienable right or a staggering responsibility.

Until recently, most working and retired Americans viewed healthcare coverage as a given—something we received through our employers simply by virtue of being employed, or from the government as a present on our 65th birthday. And it was not just that coverage was readily available. For many consumers, healthcare insurance premiums also were largely paid for by employers, and the lion's share of healthcare costs were paid by health plans or, in the case of Medicare, the federal government. As a result, the majority of us have spent most of our lives without having to think about the actual cost of healthcare in the context of how much value it provides. In fact, most of us would fail miserably if we were to play "The Price is Right" game if the items we were asked to price were healthcare procedures or prescription drugs.

Awareness increases as healthcare costs rise
As insurance premiums have increased at a rate much faster than general inflation, the typical employer offering healthcare benefits has shifted a portion of

this increase to employees. Consequently, consumers at all income levels have noticed a significant increase in their healthcare costs. For some consumers, increases in their portion of the healthcare insurance premium have negated any wage increases they may have achieved (or their employers have had to hold down wage increases in order to pay rising premiums). Add to this the fact that the previously insignificant office visit and pharmacy co-payments of the 1990s have also substantially increased in most places, and *deductibles*— the amount you are responsible to pay before insurance kicks in—have also gone up at a much faster rate than either inflation or average wage increases. If you have standard Medicare coverage (as opposed to Medicare Advantage), you now find you are financially responsible for costs beyond a certain range, particularly in buying prescription drugs. If you are in a subsidized program such as Medicaid, having access to healthcare has always been a fundamental aspect of your economic survival. With healthcare costs rising, its importance to you is now even greater. Suffice it to say that regardless of your economic status, your awareness of healthcare costs has increased. Although the same is true for employers, providers, brokers and health plans, this chapter concentrates on how you as a consumer might contemplate your new role as a fiscally-responsible, actively-engaged manager of your own healthcare experience?

Creating a responsibility mindset about your healthcare
Seeing healthcare as a personal responsibility will undoubtedly take some time to permeate our culture, but it is systematically imperative that we all develop this mindset. If the overall objective of the U.S. healthcare system is to optimize benefits (how healthcare is organized and paid for) and care (the delivery of high-quality results) across our entire population, then we need to put that into context for individuals and families. So, given your life stage, your health status, your economic situation and your personal values, how do you think about optimizing the benefits and care available to you and your family—that is, getting the best value for each healthcare dollar you spend? As Americans, we need to think systematically in both the short and long term, taking into account not only what choices are most convenient for us at the moment but also the implications our decisions and actions may have in terms of cost, quality and efficiency across the system. Hoping that other people are going to solve the healthcare crisis for us, either at a national or individual level, is not

a plan. Like Sarah and her family in Chapter Eight, we have to get much more actively involved.

In virtually all major areas of our lives—except in healthcare—we have a fairly solid understanding of how our actions have an impact on our life goals. For example, although we are entitled to public education through twelfth grade, we realize that how we perform during that time, coupled with the choices we make about whether and where to continue our education after high school, can have a significant impact on the quality of our lives. Most of us know that without higher education, there are certain jobs, professions and opportunities that simply won't be available to us. As a person who has been genetically disadvantaged with a major illness, I recognize that people are born with and grow up with many types of relative advantages and disadvantages that can alter the personal landscape of their lives, including the pursuit of higher education. And in using education as an example, I am sensitive to how disadvantaging factors contribute to the dismal statistics regarding high school graduation rates in our country. But, even acknowledging the inherent challenges, I think the vast preponderance of people in our country would agree that a systematic objective of our educational system is to educate students so they graduate from high school with at least a minimum set of competencies.

Similarly, in the realm of personal finances we make the connection between our actions and our life goals by deliberately trying to save money and arranging financing for major events such as college, weddings, home ownership, vacations, and retirement. In fact, one of the first pieces of systematic advice we receive as young adults entering the workforce is to begin thinking about retirement savings by contributing as much money as possible to retirement plans in a manner that maximizes our tax-deferred savings and takes advantage of any matching arrangement our employer may offer. In other words, we take disciplined action today to help create the possibility of a better financial future. We seem to understand that if we don't save a sufficient amount of money during our working lives we may not be able to retire as well, travel as much or live where we prefer to live. But we don't yet think this way in terms of healthcare.

One of these things is not like the others

When I was a kid, I watched the television show *Sesame Street*, which had a repeating musical segment entitled *One of These Things is Not Like the Others*. They showed four items, one of which just didn't fit in with the other items. Perhaps that musical game was what drove my initial interest in systems science. Little did I know then how perfectly it would sum up our nation's view of healthcare insurance relative to other important parts of our lives. So let's see how this game would play out regarding important decisions we make as adults today. When we buy homes we make monthly mortgage payments and we *also* buy homeowners insurance to protect our investment. When we buy cars we make monthly car payments and *also* buy automobile insurance in the event that we have an accident. However, the way we regard our healthcare is simply not like these other examples. When we obtain health "insurance" we make monthly premium payments for our healthcare coverage but we do not also buy separate insurance in case something were to go seriously wrong. The healthcare system most of us are familiar with is a hybrid type of insurance coverage that is expected to do the following: give us access to doctors and hospitals; provide pre-negotiated discounts when we do pay out-of-pocket (a benefit of health coverage that most people do not even think about); pay the lion's share of the normal cost of our healthcare beyond deductibles and co-payments; and provide catastrophic protection for exceptionally expensive healthcare costs.

It is important to realize that we expect much more from healthcare insurance than we do from all of the other kinds of insurance we buy. Healthcare insurance definitely is not like the others.

Despite the fact that healthcare accounts for nearly 17 percent of the U.S. gross domestic product, most working people do not consciously budget or save for the healthcare expenses they will inevitably incur out-of-pocket while employed, or later when they may no longer have health insurance through their employer. They also appear not to make a direct connection between investing in their health now, and having the quality of life they want later (including the ability to pursue other goals). As a nation, we have a substantially longer life expectancy than in decades past, and if we're fortunate to live to age sixty-five or beyond, then it is almost certain that healthcare will be one of the more expensive and time-consuming aspects of our lives. If Ben Franklin were alive today, he might be tempted to modify his famous quote to say that "in this world nothing can be said to be certain but death, taxes and *healthcare expenses.*" Given what we know about our increasing need for care as we get older, it is systematically illogical not to add healthcare to the long list of items we need to pay for each month, and for which we need to save.

Medicare may not be our safety net

While I want to steer clear of social policy in this book, a systems approach does require the consideration of social systems. Why don't most people save or plan for their healthcare expenses? For most of us, I believe there are two reasons. First, we generally know little about how the healthcare system operates and we have not been educated to think of healthcare as a financial planning category. Second, most of us assume that when we reach a certain age, the Medicare program will provide our health coverage. But it doesn't really matter whether we believe that health coverage in our senior years is an inalienable right or not; from a systems perspective, it is what it is—uncertain. And just as people were shocked when the financial markets meltdown in 2008 altered their longstanding assumptions about their retirement plans, people need to consider that the government may have a significantly diminished capacity to provide healthcare benefits to our older citizens compared to what it has now. This is due in part to the fact that the Medicare system was not designed with the expectation that life expectancy would increase so significantly.

While most of us have heard that the Social Security program may run out of money, few of us know that the Medicare Part A Trust is projected to go bankrupt by 2019 (by 2016 according to some sources)[17] if things don't change. And currently, although the U.S. government does make a distinction between your retirement contributions to the Social Security system and your healthcare contributions to Medicare, the numbers are not proportionately correct given the cost of healthcare compared to other retirement expenses. Currently, we pay a 1.45 percent tax rate for Medicare and a 6.2 percent tax rate for Social Security. From a systems perspective (regardless of whether you think there should be a single-payer, government-run healthcare system or whether private insurers should continue to play a role) either the Medicare taxes will need to increase or the respective amounts of the Medicare and Social Security taxes will need to be allocated differently if we are to prevent Medicare from going bankrupt. Regardless of your perspective on social program taxation, it is clear to me that we must get more healthcare for each dollar spent by applying Integrated Healthcare Management (IHM) principles with rigor to the senior population and with extra tenacity for those seniors with multiple chronic health conditions. Doing so is both humane and fiscally responsible.

Societal responsibility: systematic education early and often
We have talked throughout this book about consumers becoming actively engaged in their own healthcare. Molly Mettler, a friend of mine who, along with her husband, Don Kemper, created a highly successful consumer healthcare content company, aptly summed up this healthcare imperative by saying, "Consumers are the greatest untapped resource in healthcare. If we want to build a better healthcare system, we must first build a better patient." I believe that this is an important and accurate statement. IHM will go a long way toward making us all better consumers by using systematic principles and information technology to drive the right information, to the right person, in the right place at the right time. However, we need to start preparing people much sooner and much more thoroughly to successfully navigate the healthcare jungle.

When I took my high school's required health class, we learned a bit about anatomy; we were taught that certain parts of our anatomy were useful for reproduction; we were lectured on how to avoid sexually transmitted diseases; and we viewed countless video clips about how illegal drugs will turn our brains into eggs in a frying pan. We also learned a little about both nutrition and personal hygiene. In speaking with high school students today, not much has changed except that now they can choose to take the class on-line, thereby avoiding the embarrassment of discussing these topics with classmates of varying maturity levels.

What if we were to modify the curriculum not just to teach the anatomical systems of the body, but also to tell students about different types of healthcare providers, about what specialists correspond with which particular human body systems, about common diseases such as diabetes and heart disease, and about the positive steps we can take in support of our own longer-term health? What if we were to introduce students to the major elements of the healthcare supply chain so they could better understand primary and preventive care, specialty care, and the general purpose of hospitals, diagnostic centers and pharmacies—giving them a chance to become intelligent healthcare consumers? And what if we were to teach them to budget healthcare into their lives as an assumed monthly expense (like food, clothing, rent and transportation) and educate them enough about the types of healthcare coverage so they would be more likely to give it some serious thought as they enter the workforce? And when these former students enter the workforce, what if we were to explain how to save for healthcare similarly to how we save for retirement? Basic education about healthcare funding mechanisms might actually encourage people to save for their healthcare expenses. If the government recognizes that there are two separate "buckets" to which people need to contribute money for their future—healthcare and retirement—then so should every consumer. But many consumers do not have the knowledge to come to this conclusion on their own. Comprehensive education starting when people are young and continuing into their early adulthood makes systematic sense if we expect consumers to understand and actively engage in important decisions about their health and healthcare expenses over a lifetime.

Personal responsibility: Your behavior affects your bottom line

By now you must have a sense of how I would answer the opening questions of this chapter. Healthcare is most definitely a responsibility. But it is also an opportunity. If you take the view that as you get older there is a good chance you will need more medical care, then expecting your government to take care of all your healthcare needs for the rest of your life is essentially playing a high-risk game. Proactively planning for your future healthcare needs is the only way to ensure that you will be able to pay for your healthcare in your later years. Similarly, it is incumbent upon all of us to look at our behaviors as they relate to our health. We must accept the fact that if we fail to stop smoking, if we do not keep our weight down or commit to regular exercise, or if we choose other behaviors shown by evidence-based medicine to adversely affect our health, then we may need more care and it is systematically logical that we might be expected to pay more for our healthcare. And when it comes to understanding the cost of healthcare, we each need to take on a more retail-oriented mindset. In other words, by learning how much different components of healthcare actually cost and creating a culture of health where each of us is conscious of the value we receive for each healthcare dollar spent, we will all help drive greater efficiency in healthcare just as we have in other industries. Moreover, by taking responsibility for our day-to-day behaviors and healthcare spending, along with financial planning for future healthcare needs, we have the opportunity to influence whether we achieve our lifelong goals.

On the healthcare horizon

Of course, as I know far too well, there are many people who are genetically disadvantaged and, through no fault of their own, will require more care at greater cost than others. The healthcare system must be designed to allow for these cases in which the medical needs of individuals cannot be controlled or determined by their behaviors, and to ensure that these people are not excluded from organized systems of benefits and care. While it is true that taking care of people with significant chronic illness is relatively expensive, it will be even more expensive in total if we wait for catastrophic things to occur, which is often the case when people are excluded from coverage for pre-existing conditions. The good news, however, is that because the medical research component of our healthcare system is so sophisticated, over time people who have been "genetically picked on" will have more weapons with which to fight back. And by using IHM principles to help identify and segment consumers into groupings that can systematically give them the best information and evidence-based care available, we can deliver a high-quality healthcare experience to more people.

On the brink of unmitigated success

I will leave it to the philosophers and policymakers to calculate the cost of a human life and to determine how much should be spent to save it. But I will say that if we apply Integrated Healthcare Management principles to the U.S. healthcare system, our overall health status will improve, we will spend less and receive better care for each dollar spent, and we will free up more money for policymakers to determine how to spend or save.

As Integrated Healthcare Management enters the marketplace as a basis for reforming our healthcare system in a sustainable and affordable way, you should expect and demand the following:

- Greater transparency on the actual price of healthcare services, drugs and supplies

- Benefits that are tailored or personalized for you and members of your family

- A regularly updated health improvement plan and aligned incentives among you and your physicians to support its accomplishment

- A personal health record containing demographic, health history and benefits data populated by your health plan that is under your control for purposes of granting access and transportable if you change health plans

- Physician office and hospital clinical systems that apply electronic medical records and electronic health records for improved quality, efficiency, and patient safety

- A more cooperative and less adversarial relationship between your health plan and your providers, who will work in concert on your behalf

- More reliance on evidence-based medicine in making informed decisions about your care

- Personal responsibility on your part for your controllable health behaviors, your health decisions, and your current and longer-term healthcare financial planning

- Technologically enhanced dialogue (relevant to your health status, economic status and life stage and personal values) through social networks between consumers and providers

Conclusion—Let's Get Moving

We are at a critical juncture for healthcare in the United States. By following the systematic principles of Integrated Healthcare Management (IHM), we are poised to be able to solve our affordability and quality crisis in a sustainable way. By having a framework that recognizes that health benefits (i.e., coverage) and the spectrum of care (i.e., treatment, prevention, health and wellness) must be coordinated among constituents, we can address access issues for the uninsured, under-insured and insured. That is because IHM addresses the root causes that perpetuate today's misaligned incentives and looks at healthcare as a total system. And IHM does so in a way that can build upon today's public and private system. Realistically, we could not realign a $2 trillion-plus industry without connecting current realities to IHM's future framework. Every system must be designed and structured to achieve a particular goal—and no matter what our social policy with regard to levels of funding—we must pursue the goal of creating the greatest healthcare value for each healthcare dollar we spend. Like other industries, we must adopt a mindset that the value we expect for each healthcare dollar spent will continuously increase over time, and that the same things will not just go up in price each year.

We built the definition of IHM with the consumer as the focal point, and with the acknowledgement that the consumer is on the demand side of a complex supply chain. At TriZetto, we define IHM as *the systematic application of processes and shared information to optimize the coordination of benefits and care for the healthcare consumer.* You now know, from reading this book, that consumers, providers, employers, brokers and payers (health plans) are all constituent components of this system, and you have a better understanding of how different processes, applied technologies, information technology and behaviors work today and will need to work differently as we move toward IHM. In the earlier chapters, I explained a number of activities that health plans and providers in particular must undertake and partner on to achieve IHM. Chapter Ten is meant to emphasize that even if all the other constituents do these things, we as healthcare consumers must be actively engaged. It is the duty of our society to educate consumers early and often about the important role healthcare and its associated expense play throughout our lives. And as consumers, it is up to us to actively participate in our healthcare decision-making and to plan for the day-to-day expenses and future costs we hope to live long enough to incur.

Just imagine the best of benefits administration and the best of care management converging at the right place, at the right time, to optimize your own healthcare while also systematically improving our nation's healthcare system as a whole. I see that IHM places this future imminently within our grasp.

Acknowledgments

In my experience, few people read acknowledgements. I hope this one is read.

After a reasonably healthy childhood, I was "blessed" with a challenging and painful illness, Crohn's disease, as I was in the midst of my college education. I carried this blessing into my marriage, through my early working years and into fatherhood. Somehow, I arrived as a young adult in a time where digital computing and communications technology, accounting, cost management, process management, information management, and re-engineered industry models explosively converged. In my early career at Andersen Consulting (now Accenture), I was invested in, and given a chance to explore multiple industries such as banking, mining and manufacturing, and multiple functions such as accounting, finance, operations, marketing, and sales. As I began to specialize as a consultant in the healthcare industry, I met a group of people, many of whom I am still privileged to work with today.

Still very ill and in daily physical pain and discomfort, I became entrenched in the healthcare industry at the advent of managed care. I lived it first hand, as I helped run it at Comprecare, TakeCare and FHP. I was handed the reins of information technology in increasingly large organizations by CEOs who had the courage to support a very young executive. And I was surrounded by inventors, trying to figure out how you could create affordable, accessible and high-quality health care in a manner that wouldn't break the bank of employers and consumers. We tried many ideas, and many of them worked while some of them failed. I learned that failure was most often a result of highly-capable people pitting themselves against one another as equal and opposing forces. And I learned that my role—even though I was regarded as the "systems" guy, was to converge ideas that seemed irreconcilable. You gain the perspective to do this if at 8:00 a.m. you are debating a group of physicians about data quality; at 10:00 a.m. you are reviewing an electronic medical record implementation; at 2:00 p.m. you are designing ways to properly reimburse primary care physicians for the increased value they bring; and at 11:00 p.m. you literally are having your life saved by a surgeon and gastroenterologist working together on your behalf while the anesthesiologist (knowing my background) inquires about aspects of managed care reimbursement while putting me under.

And so my first acknowledgment is to all of the people I have encountered who are good at what they do, are set in their ways, and do not easily change their perspectives. You each inspire me to create fusion—so much more powerful than divisive behavior—when fission is the status quo.

Then, of course, there is this book—*The Information Cure*. It is an inadequate but encompassing synthesis that is intended to help people take a step back from a very complex challenge, and then step back in to attack it again. While I have tried to articulate principles that have been vetted over 25 years, I intend to keep learning by listening to the viewpoints of all constituents. The book would never have resulted in a fully written form without the collaboration of Karin Leinwand, who patiently made sure that the words on the page expressed their intended meaning. Hugh Kennedy kept us on point and reminded us that we needed to turn the ideas into a consumable deliverable. Laura Fitzgerald, as she has been for years, was my metronome. Linda Bernier's rare intellect and good humor kept us sane. Contributors, reviewers and fact checkers included David Algeo, Larry Bridge, Debi Curbey, Stephen Furia, Eric Grossman, Dave Pinkert, Brad Samson, Jim Sullivan, Tom Main, Mike Watkins, and my longtime business associate and friend—and an IHM progenitor in his own right—Dan Spirek.

My wife, daughters and extended family make all efforts to improve the world worthwhile.

To Integrated Healthcare Management!

– Jeff

Notes

1. United States Census Bureau (2007)
2. AOL, http://members.aol.com/Wildlifer/blindmen.htm
3. "Physicians in primary care and subspecialties by gender." American Medical Association. (March 10, 2008). http://www.ama.org/ama/pub/category/2687.html.
4. "Fast Facts on US Hospitals." American Hospital Association Resource Center. (October 23, 2007). http//www.aha.org/aha/resource-center/Statistics-and-Studies/fast-facts.html.
5. "Prescription Drug Trends." Kaiser Family Foundation. (September 2008). http://www.kff.org/rxdrugs/upload/3057_07.pdf
6. "Health Insurance Costs." National Coalition on Health Care. http:// www.nchc.org/facts/cost.shtml
7. See http://www.dartmouthatlas.org
8. Insurance Department Resources Report 2006 edition, National Association of Insurance Commissioners
9. Williamson JD, Danaher K: Self Care in Health. London: Croom Helm Publishing, 1978
10. "AMA works to reverse primary care physician shortage," American Medical Association, (November 10, 2008), http://www.ama-assn.org/ama/pub/category/print/20276.html
11. Ibid
12. Insurance Department Resources Report, NAIC, Table 26. See Note 8.
13. Surgical Decision Making for Degenerative Spinal Disorders: Small area analysis of surgery for low back pain. Spine 1992;17:575–9. Keller RB, Soule DN, Wennburg JE, et al.].
14. Study by Thomas J. Main. Partner and U.S. Market Leader, Oliver Wyman Health and Life Sciences. All Rights Reserved.
15. See http://content.nejm.org/cgi/content/full/NEJMsa0802005
16. President Barack Obama, White House Forum on Health Reform, Washington, D.C., March 5, 2009.
17. See http://www.healthimaging.com, CMS: Economic crisis may break Medicare by 2016 (January 20, 2009), p. 1

Book illustrations by Jonathan Evans